IF YOU WANT TO BE THE GLAMOUR GIRL
OF YOUR DAYDREAMS

McCall's

Guide to Teen-age Beauty and Glamour

tells you how to come face-to-face with yourself and
recast your own image

► *You'll find out how to*

- **CHANGE YOURSELF FROM A SLOUCH TO A SYLPH**
  (just exercise daily)

- **ACQUIRE GOOD LOOKS**
  (beautify skin and hands)

- **WEAR CLOTHES LIKE A MODEL**
  (plan your wardrobe to enhance your
  appearance)

- **SCORE HIGH ON PERSONALITY**
  (develop tact, poise, and animation)

- **KEEP WELL INFORMED**
  (beauty and brains *can* go together)

- **BE RELAXED ON DATES**
  (frank but not frantic)

Here is the road to glamour mapped out step by
step in detail. You have only to make this routine
a daily part of your life, and you can attain a charm
and radiance that will make you a stand-out where-
ever you go and the most popular girl in your set.

McCall's
Guide to Teen-age Beauty & Glamour

by

BETSY KEIFFER

Illustrated by Sheila Greenwald

PYRAMID BOOKS • NEW YORK

McCALL'S GUIDE TO TEEN-AGE BEAUTY AND GLAMOUR

A PYRAMID BOOK—published by arrangement with Prentice-Hall, Inc.

PRINTING HISTORY—Prentice-Hall edition published September 1959
Second printing . . . . October 1959
Third printing . . . . April 1960
Fourth printing . . . . April 1960
Fifth printing . . . . August 1960
Sixth printing . . . . January 1961
Seventh printing . . . . . . February 1962
Pyramid edition published October 1963
Second printing . . . . January 1965
Third printing . . . . April 1965

Library of Congress Catalog Card Number 59-14146

Printed in the United States of America

PYRAMID BOOKS are published by Pyramid Publications, Inc.,
444 Madison Avenue, New York, N.Y. 10022, U.S.A.

McCall's

Guide to Teen-age Beauty and Glamour

Contents

Introduction

Not too long ago I believed in miracles—such miracles as changing your personality overnight, losing weight without dieting, suddenly becoming the most popular girl in the crowd, having the answers to a tough exam "come to you" even though you never cracked a book. I was awfully disappointed when none of these miracles happened to me.

Since then I've learned that they almost never happen to anyone else, either. No matter what it is we want—a good figure, an exciting job, a pleasing personality or more dates than we can handle—we have to work at getting it. And I have learned something else that's equally important: if we really make up our minds to do something, we can almost always do it. No one else can do it for us, though often they can tell us how to do it.

That is what I hope to tell you in this book. If there are

things about yourself that you want to change or improve, you and only you can do it. But perhaps I can tell you how to do what you want to do to make yourself the person you want to be.

Before anyone can get along happily with other people, she must get along happily with herself. By that I mean she must basically approve of herself and have the quiet confidence that comes from knowing that though she may not be perfect in every respect, she has done as much to improve herself as any human being can reasonably do.

The girl who wails, "Look at me, I'm just hopeless," is likely to find the rest of the world hopeless too. No miracle is going to change the situation. Until she stops wailing long enough to face her problems honestly and try to solve them, she'll go right on being miserable.

So, before you read any further than this page, ask yourself, "How do I like *me*?" Take stock, first of yourself from head to toe in a full-length mirror, then of your personality, your talents, your ideas. Are you perfectly satisfied on every count? If you are, you're a lucky girl.

But if, like poor "hopeless," you feel there are just too many things wrong to enumerate, the chances are you're not being fair to yourself. Every one of us in this world has assets and handicaps, good features as well as bad. It may help you to make a list of both.

If you can't trust your own appraisal of yourself, ask someone else to help you make the list. Perhaps you could talk it over with your mother or sister or with some girl you admire. But be sure to ask the help of someone whose opinion you truly respect and whom you can trust to be honest and fair in her appraisal of you.

Once you learn what it is about yourself that needs improving, there's no longer any reason to feel helpless or hopeless. You have an objective now, so start working on it. And you'll find one kind of miracle that actually does exist—the miracle of how much we can accomplish once we make up our minds to try.

Part 1

The Way You Look

1. Problems with Figures

How many times have you watched one of your school friends who is a good thirty pounds heftier than she should be plunge her spoon into a marshmallow-fudge-nut sundae, groaning as she does so, "Oh, I *shouldn't!* There must be at least five hundred calories in this." Whereupon, with a few more sighs about her weight, she scrapes the last delicious spoonful off the side of the dish and goes home to sit down to a three-course dinner.

Who is she kidding? Not you, certainly. But obviously she is kidding herself. She must either have the idea that if she feels guilty enough when she eats it won't make her fat, or she's trying to persuade herself she really isn't too fat; or she doesn't care sufficiently about the fact that she *is* too fat to stop overeating, but hasn't quite got the courage to admit it. Well, nothing about this girl's looks is going to change for the better until she stops deluding herself and faces honestly what she is and what she wants to be.

If you have a figure problem—and even some of the most glamorous fashion models do—there is only one way to handle it. Admit it exists, find out what can be done to correct it, do all you can—and then stop fretting! I add that last because other people (and you're fretting on their account) are rarely as conscious of flaws in our appearances as we are ourselves.

So let's start out with a long, unhurried, honest look in the full-length mirror. To make your appraisal easier, here is a check list of the most common figure problems:

▶ Too Heavy

This is one it's very hard to ignore. If the mirror doesn't tell you, the straining seams of your clothes will —and your schoolmates probably already have. Being too fat is no fun, nor is it something for other people to make fun of. But wishing or weeping won't take off those pounds. Only a real, sustained, long-term effort will do it. Hard work, but it *does* pay off.

Will power, common sense and patience are your best weapons for licking the overweight problem. There is no such thing as a diet that allows you to eat all you please and still lose unneeded pounds. There is no trick, no miracle. Anything that sounds like an "easy way to lose pounds" probably isn't all that easy. But if you want to lose weight you can. And even if you don't want to, you should—for the sake of your health and happiness as well as your appearance.

The first step is to talk to a doctor, your family physician or the school doctor. This is extremely important for several reasons. *You* may think you're too heavy, but only a trained person can tell you whether you really are and, if so, how much too heavy. What you take as an indication that you're going to be a mountain of fat may be normal and temporary weight for your particular stage of growth. If you are in good health and not *over*eating you'll slim down naturally without any help, and if you try to force the process you run the risk of making yourself sick.

However, if your doctor agrees that you *are* overweight, he is the proper person to decide how much you should lose and in what length of time and by what means. By yourself, you might decide to aim for some particular weight, only to find to your disappointment that it is completely unattainable for a person of your height and bone structure. Your doctor is also the person to decide at what rate you should lose those pounds. Don't think it can be done in a matter of days. Though it is possible, by starving yourself, to lose as much as six pounds in two or three days, it is also a complete waste of time. Weight lost that fast is sure to come back as quickly as it went, and nowadays doctors know a great deal more about the ways in which these sudden changes in weight can damage health and even shorten life.

It is also best, if possible, to let your doctor prescribe your diet, since he knows you, your problems and your eating habits. But if you want to take tips from the sample menus at the end of this chapter, ask him to look them over. He may also be able to suggest some exercises to help you stay firm as your weight goes down or to trim off inches in especially bulgy places. If not, you'll also find exercises for that purpose at the end of this chapter. Needless to say, exercise and fresh air are as important as diet to your regimen, since weight depends not only on what we eat but also on how much energy we burn up.

Finally, six commandments for happy and successful dieting:

1. Don't skip breakfast, ever! When you're cutting down your total daily intake, it's a more important meal than ever. There are plenty of breakfast menus that are not fattening and that will get your day off to a proper start.

2. Don't try to kill your appetite with pills, unless they are prescribed by your doctor. If you do, you're wasting your money and courting illness.

3. Don't try to use black coffee or cigarettes as substitutes for food. You might lose some weight on such a diet, but you'd also lose your looks.

4. Do equip yourself with a calorie counter. You need it to plan practical, well-balanced meals. Besides, it makes dieting more like a game.

5. If you're always hungry, try non-fattening nibbles between meals to take the edge off your appetite. A sensible snack such as a carrot, apple, small hard candy or glass of skim milk taken an hour or so before a meal may help you stick to your diet.

6. Do use some imagination about your diet. It needn't

be deadly dull or wildly expensive or hopelessly bizarre. See how many good-tasting non-fattening dishes you can think up and ask your mother to help you fit your diet plan in with family meals. She'll be more than glad to when she sees you're serious about your program.

One of the things that makes dieting easier to stick with is knowing that it's going to end. Why don't you fill out the weekly weight record at the end of this chapter, and if you stick to your regimen faithfully, when the time limit you and your doctor set has passed, you'll be able to look in the mirror and see the girl you want to see. It's a goal worth striving for.

▶ *Too Thin*

Skirt bags, sweater sags, stockings wrinkle around the ankle? Ashamed to be seen in a bathing suit? Famous in the family as a "picky eater"? Almost certainly you're too thin, not that it's really any news to you. You've probably been answering to "Skinny" ever since you can remember. If you want to do something about it, the way to start is to find out from your family or school doctor just how much too thin you are and how much

weight you can reasonably expect to add. Though the overweight girl would dispute it with her dying breath, it is a fact that it's harder to put on weight than to lose it. But it can be done, as you will see.

If you've been underweight for some time, I'd be willing to bet that you're also inclined to be nervous and tense, an easy target for colds, apt to be tired often, feel droopy and look it much of the time. No, I'm not clairvoyant, but the vicious cycle that goes with being seriously underweight is well known. What happens is this: the very thin person is usually constitutionally nervous and high-strung. She finds it hard to relax and to rest. As a result, she burns up her energy faster than she can replace it. Result of that: she tires easily, is susceptible to infection and hasn't an appetite worthy of a mouse.

So, clearly, your first step, once you have checked with your doctor to make sure your general health is good, is to try to relax. One way to do this is to get eight or nine hours' sleep *every* night. Yes, I mean it, for the simple reason that the more tired you are, the harder it is to relax, and the less relaxed you are the harder it is to get rested—another vicious cycle.

Your second step is to make up your mind to the fact that your birdlike appetite may be the result of habit as much as anything. So try to leave "But I'm not hungry" and "I don't feel like eating now" out of your vocabulary for a few months, and concentrate instead on pleasant ways to step up the food values of what you do eat. Here are a few, and your own ingenuity should supply more:

1. Use lots of extra butter on your bread and vegetables.

2. Drink half-and-half instead of plain milk. If you dislike the taste of milk, try adding a few drops of vanilla, chocolate syrup, or some other flavoring you do like to it.

3. Add dried fruits like raisins, apricots, prunes to your hot cereal at breakfast. Or slice a banana into cold cereal.

4. Add powdered milk to milkshakes, cream soups, hot cereals.

5. At the end of this chapter you will find "Menus for Weight Gainers" to help guide you in eating the way you need to if you want to add pounds.

Another easy way to increase your food intake each day is with snacks. Chances are, your appetite is somewhat smaller than average already, and the thought of tucking away a tremendous meal is appalling to you. So eat normal-sized meals and supplement them with lots of small snacks. Try to have a mid-morning, mid-afternoon and before-bed snack every day. Be sure that the first two are at least two hours before regular mealtime and make them as hearty as possible: a cup of cocoa and two oatmeal cookies in midmorning, perhaps; a malted or ice cream soda in the afternoon; an eggnog with cookies before you go to bed.

Now that we have ticked off sleep, relaxation, and food as vital to gaining weight—and vital to staying healthy, for that matter—let's add two more equally vital factors: fresh air and exercise. These two are so easy to come by we often forget they're available and important.

Anyone who spends most of her waking and sleeping hours in a stuffy room is all too likely to feel dopey, listless and totally disinclined to eat. An open window in the bedroom at night is a must, and so is at least an hour in the fresh air, barring hailstones, blizzards and downpours.

To many, exercise is a dirty word, but it needn't be. Exercise needn't mean strenuous games, if you hate them, or strenuous calisthenics. Walking is good exercise, helping with the housework is exercise, riding a bike and mowing the lawn are exercise, lots of hobbies are exercise, and a daily dozen can be exercise with a very worthwhile purpose—strengthening special muscles to improve your figure.

Finally, in your pound-adding regimen, you need a calorie counter to plan your meals sensibly. Once you or your doctor have figured out the amount of calories you have been eating, he can tell you how many more it would be reasonable to add to your diet. Don't be discouraged because you can't consume the total number at the beginning. Like losing weight, adding it is a gradual process, but it will certainly repay you with twice the looks, twice the energy and half the colds you were blessed with before.

Meanwhile, some beauty and fashion tips: even though it may take a bit of doing, work out a hair style that doesn't hug your head, accentuating your look of thinness. If your hair is fine and hard to handle, a soft permanent may be needed to give it the body for soft, full hairdos. Use clothes to "pad out" your proportions: textured fabrics, easy-fitting styles, diagonal or horizontal stripes, full skirts, bulky sweaters and jackets, bright colors will all help to give an illusion of fullness where it is needed.

▶ *Too Tall or Too Short*

Since inches can't be lopped off like pounds, there's nothing you can do to make yourself shorter. But there are several things you can *stop* doing if you have the mistaken impression that they camouflage your height. You can stop slouching, hanging your head and fidgeting with your hands because you feel self-conscious about

letting your arms hang. Remember that you're too tall only if you *feel* too tall. Carried with poise, your height can give you a distinction the short girl will never attain. The secrets of this are posture and clothes.

The tall girl who is blessed with a good figure is also blessed with the ability to wear a greater variety of styles and more dramatic styles than most girls. So make the most of your proportions with bold prints, off-beat colors, wide, wide belts, skinny pants. Minimize your height with horizontal lines, contrast belts, skirts and tops of different colors, medium-heeled shoes (flats don't make you *that* much shorter, so don't feel you must stick to them).

Concentrate on relaxing gracefully, and holding yourself proudly. Don't huddle when you sit, don't feel you must keep your elbows bent or your hands moving nervously because you think your arms look "too long" when they hang at your sides. They don't—when they hang naturally. Read the section on posture, which follows. There are tips for you in it.

If you are short, choose your wardrobe with care, for clothes spell much of the difference between seeming attractively petite and just plain "half-pint."

Stick to dresses that are simple, that accentuate the vertical and that are in proportion with your proportions. Tall girl styles won't make you seem taller; they'll only make you look like a small girl wearing a big girl's clothes. Leave the big prints, bold plaids, broad stripes, wide belts and bulky styles for the Junos. Be feminine but not fussy in accessories and jewelry. And watch your figure! There's less of you to spread extra pounds over.

► *Poor Posture*

A universal human weakness is our tendency to convince ourselves that if we don't see something it doesn't exist. There are probably more people in the world with poor posture than with any other figure problem, but few who try to correct it. They may not see how they look, but everyone else does, unfortunately. And, sadder still, round shoulders or head sunk on breastbone can ruin the looks of even the most breathtaking figure. Bad posture isn't a hard fault to correct, but it will never be done by just that automatic straighten-up-slouch-down-again every time Mother says, "For Heaven's sake, sit up!"

If *your* stance is as droopy as last week's rose, there must be a reason for it. So step one in this case is to pinpoint the reason. Do you slouch because you think it will make you look shorter? Do you slump because you're too tired to straighten up? Do you hunch your shoulders and poke your head forward in an effort to see better? Are you permanently thrown off balance by constant wearing of too-high heels?

If you're honest with yourself, you should be able to supply the reason for your less than perfect posture—and remove it. If you *are* tired all the time, see what treating yourself to a reasonable amount of sleep—at least eight hours every night—will do for you. If after a few weeks you don't find yourself feeling fresher, you may need to talk to a doctor.

If you have had the idea that slumping will make you look shorter, forget it. It simply calls attention to your height. If faulty vision is the reason behind it all, break down and wear your glasses—they're more becoming than a turtle-like stance—or, if you haven't any and suspect you need them, consult an oculist. And if your shoes are at the root of the trouble, save the spike heels for dates and choose something comfortable for daily wear. No woman can look her best when her feet hurt, anyway.

Now, with the cause of the problem accounted for, it's time to take positive action. You will have to remind yourself to sit and stand properly at least a dozen times a day. This does *not* mean wrenching back your shoulders and thrusting out your derrière so that your figure describes an S instead of the C it did when you slumped. Good posture calls for straight shoulders, rib cage pulled up, tummy and fanny tucked in, knees flexed naturally. You'll see how important that last is if you try to stand gracefully with your knees stiff. It just can't be done.

To sit and stand correctly for more than two minutes at a time, you will have to strengthen your muscles. Ten minutes a day of the right exercises—and it must be *every* day—will help immeasurably. You'll find exercises for the purpose at the end of this chapter. Don't expect miracles from them. You won't be standing straight as an arrow in a few days, perhaps not even in a few weeks. But if you are patient and faithful, it won't be too long before you overhear someone say, "Doesn't she carry herself beautifully?"

One dividend you may reap along the way: as soon as you begin to stand straighter, you're likely to be rewarded with a nearer handspan waist. The thickened waistline, rudely called a "jelly roll," is often the result of poor posture. A quick way to find out if this is the case: slip a tape measure around your waist when you're standing naturally (and no cheating, please!) and compare the inches with your measurement when you pull up your rib cage and hold your shoulders straight. If you also have more flesh than you need around the waist, combine the exercises for waist and abdomen with those for general posture.

▶ Bosom—Too Much or Too Little

If you have a problem in this department, the chances are that it's neither so grave nor so permanent as you think it is. For one thing, your proportions are still changing, and what seems like an opera star's endowment today may be in perfect proportion with the rest of you by the time you're in your twenties. And what strikes you as a calamitously flat chest still has time to develop more becoming contours. But in either case there are ways to make yourself happier about your looks in the meantime.

If you think your bosom is too large, and you are not generally overweight, clever camouflage is your best ally. Your bra is an essential ingredient of this. Shop in a store that has a wide selection, enlist the help of a sales-girl—because they know more about this problem than you do—and find a well-designed bra that really fits and supports. Remember that your clothes, too, make a world of difference in the total effect. Stay away from tight sweaters, extravagant collars or necklines, and blouses or dresses made of nubby materials or such clinging fabrics as jersey. Full skirts and waists not too tightly belted will help you look well proportioned. Another point: avoid the sort of hairdo that adds to a top-heavy effect. Keep your hair medium length, simple and sleek. And please, please, don't hunch over. You have nothing to hide.

If your problem is just the opposite, a bit of padding in your bra, otherwise known as a "falsie," is nothing to be ashamed of. But do choose both bra and pad (some bras come with built-in padding) carefully. Make sure you're comfortable and look natural. Experiment with clothes until you find a cut—often a bias top—that accents your bosom becomingly. For casual wear, stick to blouses or bulky sweaters instead of skin-tight pull-overs.

Naturally, if you look flat-chested because you're too thin, it's only sensible to try to put on some weight. And exercises, though there are none which will develop the breasts themselves, can strengthen the muscles that support them and help you avoid a caved-in look. My final plea: don't waste money on so-called "developing" creams or lotions. The one that really works has yet to be invented.

▶ *Hips*

Like bosoms, if they're in style one year, they're sure to be out of style the next. So whether you're slim as a reed or shaped like an hourglass, there's bound to be some year when your figure is fashionable. But if you are too "hippy" and this is your off-year in fashion's eyes, don't just wait patiently for the next one to roll around. Give yourself a good firm poke. What's the hippiness made of? Bones or too much flesh? Bones can't be shaved, but too much flesh can, whether it's part of a general overweight pattern or just your particular tragedy that everything you eat seems to go to your hips. If it is the latter problem, try the exercises for hips at the end of this chapter. But remember, doing them a couple of times a week is just no good at all. To get results, you must do them *every* day for lots of days.

Meanwhile, before you do become a sylph, don't wear your belts tight to show off your tiny waist; the comparison makes your hips look all the larger. Don't wear skirts or dresses in bold colors or violent patterns. Stay away from plaids, unless they are cut on the bias, and from dirndls and from skirts that hug you tight. Above all, rule shorts and slacks out of your wardrobe. They were never meant for the hourglass figure.

► **Legs**

There is probably no other country in the world where people are as conscious of legs as they are in the United States. We've so completely forgotten that legs are to get around on that a girl who isn't blessed with stems like Marlene Dietrich's feels she has suffered a monumental tragedy. She hasn't really, but if *you* feel the appearance of your legs might be improved on, there *are* ways.

Whether your leg problem is "too much" or "too little," both diet and exercise can help to a certain extent. Neither, naturally, is going to transform your legs into million-dollar assets unless the basic structure is there. But obviously, taking off weight will help the looks of too-heavy legs, and putting it on will improve too-thin ones. And there are exercises which can improve circulation and help redistribute fatty tissues, as well as build up the calf muscles to give legs more contour. You will find them at the end of this chapter.

There are other points to bear in mind, too, in either case: shoes and stockings in extreme colors will call attention to your legs; seamless stockings add width, which means they're a help for skinny legs, unbecoming to heavy ones; skirt length is very important (find the length most flattering to you—usually it covers the thickest part of the calf—and stick to it, no matter what capricious fashion dictates); and be sure that your legs are perfectly groomed, always—meaning smooth-skinned and de-fuzzed.

Now you have gone down to the head-to-toe check list, faced your problem, if you have one, and found out what to do about it. I doubt that you checked none of the problems or that you checked all, but there is a good chance that if you checked several they are related.

The girl who is overweight is almost sure to be afflicted with big hips, heavy legs, an oversize bosom. That picky eater is probably the one who checked no front, and skinny legs. The girl who thinks she is too tall is also the girl who goes around with her head scrunched into her shoulder blades and her back curved like a bow.

But if any of these is you, don't be discouraged by the number of problems you have to work on. Because once you have solved the basic problem, the others will most likely take care of themselves.

And now that you have given your figure such a thorough going-over, it's time to move on to your face.

▶ *Menus for Calorie Counters*

To prove my point that calories—and not fads—are the clue to weight, I submit two sets of menus. Basically, you'll see, they are the same menu, but if you chose your breakfast, lunch and dinner from the left-hand side of the page you'd be eating about 1100 calories a day —the number that's usually recommended for losing weight; and if you followed the menus on the right-hand side you'd be eating just about twice that number of calories. If gaining is what you're after, the right-hand side, plus around eight hundred calories of in-between snacks, is for you.

The other point these menus make, I hope, is that there's no reason a dieter shouldn't eat in happy harmony with the rest of the family. No special weird dishes or exotic menus need be prepared for her. Restraint, bolstered by non-fattening snacks before meals if necessary, is all she needs.

Breakfast for weight losers	*Breakfast for weight gainers*
½ tangerine	1 tangerine
1 soft-boiled egg	⅔ cup hot cereal with sugar, cream
1 slice toast	
Buttermilk or skim milk (1 glass)	Scrambled eggs on buttered toast
	1 glass milk
or	or
1 orange	1 cup orange juice
½ cup cold cereal with sugar, skim milk	1 cup cold cereal with brown sugar, cream
Tea with sugar	Buttered English muffin
	Hot chocolate

Breakfast for weight losers	*Breakfast for weight gainers*
or	or
½ grapefruit 2 strips bacon 1 slice plain toast 1 glass buttermilk or skim milk	1 cup grapefruit juice 1 fried egg with 2 strips bacon 1 slice buttered toast with jam Hot chocolate

Lunches for weight losers	*Lunches for weight gainers*
Toasted cheese sandwich (1 slice bread) 1 small apple Buttermilk or skim milk	Toasted cheese & bacon sandwich (2 slices bread) Vegetable salad with mayonnaise 1 large apple, 2 cookies 1 glass milk
or	or
Sandwich: 1 slice each of ham, cheese, rye bread Fresh pear Skim milk or buttermilk	Ham & cheese sandwich with 2 slices buttered bread Baked apple with cream Vanilla milkshake
or	or
Frankfurter with mustard, no roll 2 salted crackers 1 medium orange	Frankfurter with mustard on roll 1 cup cabbage salad with mayonnaise

Dinners for weight losers

Dinners for weight gainers

1 glass buttermilk or skim milk

Medium piece of pie
1 glass milk

1 medium hamburger, no bun
½ small baked potato with butter
⅔ cup cabbage salad with lemon juice
½ cup fruit cocktail
1 glass buttermilk or skim milk

1 medium hamburger with bun
1 baked potato with sour cream
½ cup buttered peas
1 cup cabbage salad with dressing
⅔ cup fruit cocktail, 2 cookies
1 glass milk

or

or

Small serving roast chicken
½ small baked potato with butter
½ cup plain green beans
Green salad with lemon juice
Small serving cake
1 glass iced tea

Medium serving roast chicken with gravy
½ cup French fried potatoes
1 cup buttered green beans
Green salad with dressing
Angel food cake with whipped cream
1 glass milk

or

or

Broiled fish fillet
Small potato with butter
½ cup plain broccoli

Broiled fish fillet with tartar sauce
2 small potatoes with butter

Dinners for weight losers	Dinners for weight gainers
Lettuce salad with lemon	½ cup buttered broccoli
2 fig cookies	Lettuce salad with French dressing
Buttermilk or skim milk	Vanilla ice cream, 2 fig cookies
	Milk

▶ Sixteen Figure Tamers

Good posture is really the master key to a good figure, because often the proportions that seem out of whack are actually out of place—the prominent tummy or derrière, the hollow chest, the double chin. Stand sideways in front of a full-length mirror, and if you can't pass the test of dropping an imaginary plumbline from the top of your head to your ankles and having it bisect your hip and knee—tackle posture first, with these:

Stand with your legs together, your knees straight. Relax forward from the waist, head down, arms down, palms facing. Swing one arm forward, the other arm back, simultaneously raising your head. Your back should be arched, shoulder blades brought together. Do two or three times the first day, working up to ten times gradually and resting at the halfway mark.

Sit on the floor with legs crossed tailor-fashion. Clasp hands behind your back. Pull down with arms and at the same time roll your shoulders back as far as possible. Let go. Repeat ten times.

Stand with feet apart, arms straight over head. Bend loosely from the waist and let your arms swing through your legs. Then swing back up to the first position. Repeat ten times, and be sure to relax completely as you do it. This general body stretch is a big help to graceful carriage.

For a better bosom: Naturally, exercises can't develop the breasts themselves, which are made up of glands and fatty tissue. But they *can* develop the chest and strengthen the muscles that support the breasts, and this, believe me, can make a tremendous difference to the fit of a sweater. Round-shouldered, flat-chested, or hollow-chested girls will be smart to:

Lie on your back with your feet together and arms straight out at the sides, palms flat on floor. Without moving your arms, raise your chest and shoulders, tilting chin so weight is on the back of your head. Relax. Do

five times, rest and repeat five times. This exercise also helps strengthen muscles of upper back and neck, so it's a posture-assister, too.

Stand with feet apart, toes turned in slightly, buttocks tucked under. Raise arms to shoulder level in front of you. Fling arms back, and then let them drop to sides.

Sit cross-legged on the floor, with arms crossed and fingertips touching shoulders. Keep your back straight and your tummy tucked in. Fling your arms up and out, stretching as far as you can. Return to first position. Repeat ten times.

Tummy-trimmers: Lie on your back with your feet flat on the floor, your knees bent. Grip thighs with both hands and *slowly* pull yourself to a sitting position. Hold it for a minute, then return to the original position. Repeat ten times.

Lie on the floor with knees bent sharply, feet flat on the floor close to buttocks, arms at sides. Slowly lift your hips as high off the floor as your can, simultaneously pulling in your abdomen; sliding your arms up over your head and tightening buttocks. With stomach still tight, return to the first position. Do four times, rest and repeat four more times.

Stand with feet apart and pointing straight ahead. Slowly raise arms over your head as high as possible; then, bending from the waist, stretch backward as far

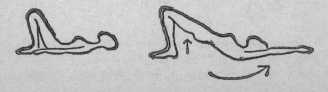

as you can without straining. Hold this position for a moment, then come forward slowly, stretching your arms ahead and keeping your knees straight until you can touch the floor with the tips of your fingers.

Note: This one takes a bit of doing. Start by doing it once or twice, work up slowly to five times. The reward —a trim and supple waistline.

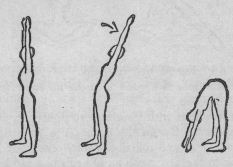

Hip shavers: Stand with your feet ten inches apart and pointing straight ahead. Grasp the right knee with your left hand; pull it up, then out to the side. Return to first position. Repeat with the left leg and right hand. Do it six times, alternating sides. This one is also good for thighs and for balance.

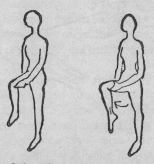

Lie on your left side, with your left arm straight up and under your head, your left hand on the floor in front of you for support. With your legs straight and your feet off the floor, scissor-kick your legs rapidly back and forth a dozen times.

Note: An exercise mat or a folded blanket between you and the floor is a good idea for all exercises, especially for this one.

Sit on the floor with your legs straight out, arms behind you, hands flat on the floor. Raise your right arm above your head and roll *slowly* over onto your left hip. Roll back to the first position. Do this one fifteen times, alternating sides.

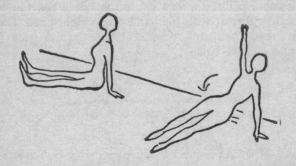

For lovelier legs: It may seem paradoxical, but the same exercise can help legs with opposite problems. Strengthening the calf muscles will give a more becoming curve to legs that are too thin, as well as better proportions to legs that are too heavy. The first two exercises here will also help heavy thighs:

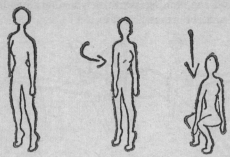

Stand, barefoot, with feet about eighteen inches apart. Rise on the balls of your feet, turn your body to the left and bend your knees, sinking down till you're almost to the floor. Straighten up and repeat, turning to the right. Do this five times, alternating sides; rest and do five more times. You'll see results in your ankles, too.

Stand with your hands on your hips, your feet apart, toes turned in. Rise on your toes, bend your knees and sink down *slowly*, pointing knees together till they touch. Come up *slowly*. *Slowly* is really the secret of this one. It's easy to do fast, but you're wasting your time if you do.

Hold on to the back of a chair for support. With your feet together, your fanny tucked under, rock back on your heels, stretching your feet and curling your toes under hard. Relax, rock again, tense your legs. Do this

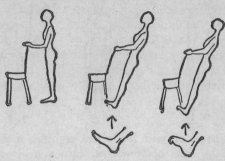

exercise ten times.

If there's figure work to be done—either addition or subtraction—keeping track of your vital statistics on this chart will show you at a glance whether your progress is something to crow about, or whether more will power is needed!

1965

Fri. Sept. 3.

Thurs.

	WEIGHT pounds	BUST Thurs. Sept. 9 inches	WAIST Thurs. Sept. 9 inches	HIPS inches	UPPER ARMS inches	THIGHS inches
At start *Sept. 9*	119	34	27	36¾		21½
End of 1st week	117					
End of 2nd week						
End of 3rd week						
End of 4th week						
End of 5th week						
End of 6th week						
End of 7th week						
End of 8th week						
End of 9th week						
End of 10th week						
End of 11th week						
End of 12th week						

110 or less   35   25   35½

You'll note it's weekly, not daily. The principal reason for this is that daily variations in weight are inevitable, but not significant. Trying to keep track of them might discourage you unnecessarily or give you a false sense of accomplishment. What is important for an accurate record is to weigh yourself on the same day of each week, at the same time of day and wearing approximately the same amount of clothes. And be sure the scales are reliable!

2. Face-to-Face with Yourself

I am going to start this chapter by being frightfully stern. What I have to say is this: if you are not willing to do right by yourself in the matters of (a) well-balanced diet, (b) enough sleep, (c) enough fresh air and exercise, you might as well stop reading right now. There is nothing in a bottle or a jar, no regimen, no technique, no trick that can make your skin lovely if you flout the fundamentals.

"All right," you may say, "but I *do* eat sensibly, I *do* get enough sleep and exercise and fresh air, and still my skin looks awful." Well, let's find out why and what you can do about it.

▶ The Common Skin Problems

Oily skin. If your face has a persistent shine, a tendency to enlarged pores, blackheads and blemishes, it means your oil glands are working overtime. In another few years they may settle down to behaving more reasonably, but meanwhile your face needs special care. Absolute cleanliness, important for the looks of any skin, is really vital in this case. You should clean your face thoroughly two or three times a day with soap and water or a non-greasy cleansing cream or lotion. If you belong to the soap-and-water school, make sure you know the technique: use warm-to-hot water and a rich lather of suds. Work them gently but thoroughly all over your face, using your fingertips or a wash cloth. Then rinse, rinse, rinse. Pat dry and follow with an astringent lotion.

Mind you, this faithful washing is not going to make the oiliness disappear. What it *will* do is guard your pores against becoming clogged with oil-plus-grime deposits, which in turn may become blackheads or blemishes.

If you have oily skin, don't use *any* oily preparations on it. After cleansing, a good astringent or skin freshener followed by a non-oily make-up is the best prescription. A smart idea: keep moistened towelettes or a tiny plastic bottle of astringent and some cotton pads in your purse to freshen your appearance quickly when you aren't able to do a real cleaning job. Or try the special tissues for your kind of skin. They blot up oil in a twinkling.

Lots of water inside, as well as outside, is also a must for oily skins. Aim for a consumption of eight glasses a day. Be sure, too, that your meals include as many fresh fruits and vegetables as possible, as few greasy foods, rich desserts and candies as your will power can manage.

And comfort yourself with this far-off thought: skin with plenty of natural oil, when it's properly cared for, will keep its freshness and youth far longer than dry skin.

Dry skin. In this case, your glands are not producing quite enough natural oils. The result: your skin chaps and flakes easily, you have a hard time keeping powder on, and your face may even feel tight and sore after washing. Poor face, it needs a little tenderness.

Clean it tenderly, but none the less thoroughly every day. To do this you may use either cleansing cream or soap and water. If you prefer the latter, it's especially vital to rinse thoroughly, since a film of soap left on your skin will dry it even more.

Make it a ritual to apply a lubricating oil, cream or lotion before you go to bed at night, and, for daytime, use a lubricant base under your make-up.

It's quite likely that the dryness problem isn't confined to your face, and likely too that it seems more acute in winter. In addition to a good diet and enough exercise, a tablespoon of oil in your nightly bath can make you feel more comfortable all over. Goodness knows there's nothing more glamorous feeling than a sweetly-scented bath oil, but if you haven't any, olive oil will do as well.

Combination skin. This is the kind of skin that is partly oily and partly dry. Nose, chin and forehead are inclined to oiliness, whereas cheeks have a tendency to be dry and flaky. It's not hard to cope with this problem. Follow the techniques for oily skin on nose, chin and forehead; go heavy on lubrication for the dry areas.

Troubled skin. If you suffer with frequent crops of blemishes, you are far from being alone. It's estimated that 90 per cent of all boys and girls in their teens have them. The chances are, too, that your skin will clear up by the time you're in your twenties, but that, I realize, is very faint comfort right now.

So don't wait for comfort; do something! And *you*, let me stress, are the one to do it. Even a doctor cannot help eruptive skin without a patient's complete cooperation. Here are the commandments you must abide by faithfully:

1. Avoid greasy foods, no matter how you love them: potato chips, French fries, salted nuts, greasy sauces, pizzas, and so on.

2. Stay away from any other categories of food that you know from experience always bring on blemishes. Chocolate, seafood, shellfish, ice cream and some cheeses are well-known troublemakers for people with disturbed skin. For you there may be others. Learn to spot them and pass them up.

3. Be *sure* you get enough sleep and enough exercise. Doctors have a strong suspicion that nervous tension makes this skin condition worse.

4. Wash your face as many times a day as you can, and be equally scrupulous about keeping your hands clean. Hands that aren't completely clean are great spreaders of infection.

5. Shampoo your hair twice a week, because it's a

safe bet your scalp is oily, and wear your hair away from your face.

6. Do not *ever* pick or squeeze a pimple. I know it's a terrible temptation, but unless you want to run the risk of causing a real infection (which can leave a permanent scar) you must resist it. Instead, use a hot compress on your face for ten or fifteen minutes before you go to bed at night. Wring out a clean face cloth in water as hot as you can stand it and hold it to your face until it cools. Repeat this several times. This softens and even carries away the blackheads that usually lead to pimples, and also brings blood to the surface of your skin to help fight bacterial infection.

7. Remember that though normal exposure to the sun is good for oily skin (the type most prone to blemishes), too much may stimulate the oil glands to even more frantic activity and make things worse.

You'll probably have noticed that so far I've not mentioned the word "acne," that dread term. The reason I haven't is that acne, a much more severe version of troubled skin and one that usually involves chronic infection, is considerably less common than you'd think from the way people toss the word around. It is also likely to require a skin doctor's care. If you really stick faithfully to the rules I've outlined at the first sign of trouble, you may find your skin clears up quickly. If it does not, you should see a doctor.

Freckles. Coming after troubled skin, freckles seem like a very minor problem, but a really spectacular crop can make you feel self-conscious. The best way to deal with them is to avoid getting them. If you are one of the freckle-prone, stay out of the sun unless you're covered up. Don't rely on sun-tan preparations to protect you; that's not what they're designed to do. Although to my knowledge there is no freckle bleach that's both effective and safe, you *can* camouflage freckles on your face by using a cake or creamy make-up base that is one or two shades darker than your skin. Once you've done all this, forget your freckles. They're usually kind of cute anyway.

▶ *Making the Most of Your Make-up*

The first question, obviously, is *what* make-up. I am not going to lay down any hard and fast rules as to the variety or amount of make-up a girl your age should wear. But I would like to suggest that you will feel most comfortable, and probably look prettiest, if you use cosmetics as the rest of the girls in your group do.

Daytime make-up usually means a powder base and powder, plus a discreet touch of lipstick, and, if you're a blonde, some deft strokes of an eyebrow pencil.

Evening and date make-up might be expanded to include mascara—and rouge, if you're really so pale that you need it.

The more exotic additions, like eye liner and eye shadow are designed for older faces. Your eyes will truly look brighter and prettier without them. But if you're determined to experiment, do make sure you master the techniques of using them. You will find tips for putting on eye make-up on pages 51-54.

Now for the essentials:

Foundation or powder base goes on first, and it goes on a *freshly-cleansed* face. Its primary purpose is to make powder stay on longer, but it can also be an invisible ally in covering skin imperfections and in protecting your skin.

If your skin is clear and your coloring good, you can use a colorless base. For pale skin, choose a shade slightly darker than your own coloring. If your skin inclines to sallowness, use a somewhat pinker tone. Foundation with a beige cast can tone down too-ruddy skin.

To put it on: stipple it lightly on your forehead, nose, cheeks and chin, then blend it in with your finger tips, using an up and out motion. The secret here: foundation must not end in an abrupt line anywhere, if it's to look natural. So be sure you carry it right to the hairline and fade it off on the neck, not the chin. Unless you want to look owl-eyed—and I know you don't—carry foundation up to meet your lower lashes and cover entire upper lid.

Rouge, if it's cream or liquid, goes on next. Remember that the whole point of rouge is to accent the *upper* part of the face. If it's carried below the tip of the nose it will give your face a pulled-down look. It's easy to put it on correctly if you use this technique: with a fingertip make two dots, one on the cheekbone beneath the center of your eye, one at the outer corner. Blend it with a clean finger, feathering it off almost to the hairline. Color cue: light shades of pink or coral are most becoming to young faces.

Dry rouge goes on after powder, but looks best with another light dusting of powder over it.

Powder, when it is put on properly, helps "set" your foundation and rouge. Never "scrub" it on. Instead, use a clean piece of cotton and "flour" your entire face and neck lavishly, smoothing off the excess wtth another bit of cotton. Tip: always use a downward stroke to make facial fuzz lie flat. If you use a colored foundation, choose powder that is one shade lighter, but be sure it's not at drastic variance with your natural skin tone.

Lipstick. You probably think you need no tips on using lipstick, but I'd be willing to bet that with a little practice you could be much more of a pro.

For example, do you own a lip brush? Do you use it successfully? If the honest answer is no, read on. A lip brush serves two important purposes: it gives your lips a well-defined line, helps prevent lipstick smearing or smudging at the edges, provided you learn to use it with a steady hand. This you do by holding the brush as though it were a pencil, resting your little finger on your chin for steadiness. Outline your lips first, starting at the corner of either lip and working toward the center. Your lips should be just slightly parted as you work. With the outline drawn (and this is where you can subtly build up a too-thin mouth, or minimize a too-full one) fill in the rest.

Important: no matter whether the current rage is for "bee-stung," "heart-shaped" or tragically drooping mouths, don't try to *alter radically* the shape of yours. The result can't help but be a clown-like look.

Give your lipstick a minute or two to set, then if it looks heavy, gently blot with a tissue. And never forget that final check in the mirror to make sure there's none smeared on your teeth. Crimson teeth, I promise, will never be in style.

Color cues: Don't forget that your lipstick shade should harmonize with your costume as well as with your coloring, and that the lighter, subtler shades have much more fashion appeal than "bleeding-heart" shades.

▶ *Your Lovely Eyes*

As I've said, in most cases eyes look their loveliest with no help at all, except possibly a light film of cold cream on the upper lid for extra sheen. But there are exceptions, I'll grant.

If you're a blonde or redhead and have the pale-to-invisible brows and lashes that go with your hair, you'll need some first-aid from eyebrow pencil and mascara. If you wear specs, you should learn some special tricks for playing up the eyes behind them. And, of course, when there's an extra-special party in view, you want to go all-out for extra-special glamour.

Your eyebrow pencil should be neither needle-sharp nor so dull it draws a heavy line. To achieve a really natural effect, first brush your brows up with a clean brush and smoothe them across the top of the arch. Then, using your pencil, fill in with short hair-like strokes. Tip: if you want to lengthen your brows, be sure the line doesn't veer up or down unnaturally. As for color, if your brows are normally pale, you'll get a more natural effect with a brown pencil.

Eye shadow comes next, and it's a smart idea to work with a magnifying mirror—particularly if you're near-sighted. Stick shadows, I think, also make the job easier. The technique: draw color on in a line as close as possible to your upper lashes, starting from about a quarter inch from the corner of the eye. With your finger tip fade it out and *up* toward the brows. If you bring it too low at the outer corners of your eyes, the result is a "closed-in" look. The color story: light eyes look brightest when they're shadowed by pastel hues. The vivid hues are more becoming to dark eyes. For glamour, the iridescent shadows are fun.

Mascara is not hard to use successfully if you keep in mind this basic rule: two light coats are far, far better than one heavy one. If your lashes stick together, it means you have forgotten it. Rule two: never put on mascara with a downward stroke; your lashes will cast an unbecoming shadow. And, of course, you use it only on your upper lashes.

If you use a brush, work the mascara well down into it, so no blobs will come off, then tilt your head back slightly and hold the brush so bristles point down, not toward your eye. This means you'll be applying mascara from the sides of the brush, not the ends of the bristles. Work from the inner to the outer corners of the eye, from the roots to the tips of lashes.

When mascara has dried, brush your lashes gently with a clean dry brush, and if you want a thicker fringe, repeat the entire operation. If your lashes are stubbornly straight, using an eyelash curler between coats of mascara can help.

P.S. The new mascara applicators are miraculously simple to use.

Eye-liner definitely takes practice to use successfully, but the technique is worth learning for those special times when you want to give your eyes a really dramatic frame. Use a soft, well-sharpened eyebrow pencil and, starting at the inner corner of the upper lid, draw a line through the base of the upper lashes ending in a slight swoop up and out at the outer corner. Note, please, that I said *"slight* sweep." That heavy, obvious line, once known as the "doe-eyed" look, is passé. Note, too, that if your eyes are very round, using an eye-liner may give them a heavy look. More becoming is an eye shadow that matches the color of your eyes.

When eye make-up is expertly used it can produce dramatic yet now clownish effects. So practice in private until you are really expert.

If you wear glasses, here are some special tricks you'll want to learn:

1. Start your eye shadow at the center of the upper lid, never at the inner corner of the eye, and fade it up and out to the brow.

2. Mascara prevents your lashes from getting lost behind your glasses. Use an eyelash curler, too, to keep them from hitting against your lenses.

3. Make the most of your brows. If they're not long enough, extend them with an eyebrow pencil.

Know how to tell how long is long enough? Hold a pencil from the corner of your nose across the outer corner of your eye. The pencil should just touch the end of your eyebrow.

Be sure that in addition to being sufficiently long and sufficiently dark, your eyebrows are perfectly groomed. That means: shape them by plucking any strays on the *under* side of the arch or over the nose; brush across the top of the arch. One caution: Don't run wild with the tweezers or you may wind up with very sparse brows or a thin, hard line that's as out of date as it is unbecoming.

3. Learning to Handle Your Hair

If you are one of the thousands of girls who have said despairingly, "I can't do a thing with my hair," strike that from the record right now. You can *so* do a thing with your hair and I hope that after you've committed to memory the tips in this chapter you'll be doing very pretty things indeed with it.

Before we even start to talk about styles and curls, let's quickly review some even more basic matters. They are: the care you take of your general health and of your hair. Very important! Because if you don't play fair with your hair, it's not going to play fair with you when you want it to look pretty.

First question: do you own a good hair brush—one with bristles that are long and firm enough to get through

your hair, but not so sharp-pointed that they scratch your scalp? Do you use said brush faithfully every day? Not just a lick and a promise, but at least one hundred strokes? (They take only four minutes.) You really must if you want to keep your hair healthy and cooperative, for it needs this stimulation to stay in good condition.

Second question: do you shampoo at least once a week and oftener if necessary? (Incidentally, it's an old wives' tale that frequent shampooing is bad for your

hair.) And do you treat yourself to a really thorough shampoo?

The technique, to cover it quickly, is as follows: first, massage your scalp with your fingertips, then thoroughly brush your entire head to loosen dry skin and

surface dirt. Wet your head completely—a spray works best for this—and apply shampoo, according to the

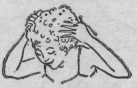

directions on the package. Work the suds in well with your fingertips before you rinse and re-suds. Keep up

your final rinsing until all your hair is "squeaky" clean, without a trace of shampoo left to make it dull or dry.

Towel it partly dry, comb it, and you're ready for your set. The whole shampoo needn't take you more than ten minutes. Then take another minute to shampoo your hairbrush and all your combs!

Faithful washing and brushing are usually all that's required to keep normal, *healthy* hair in condition. (And remember *it* won't be healthy if *you're* not.) But if you're troubled by oiliness, dryness or dandruff, you should take these special steps:

Oily hair, like oily skin, is caused by those old over-active oil glands. It's almost impossible to keep it looking pretty without special care, because the film of oil that coats it also makes it look limp and stringy.

The way to combat this problem is frequent shampooing—and you may get best results with a special oily-hair shampoo—and frequent massage-plus-brushing. Save those last ten minutes before you jump into bed at night for this routine. To make sure you're really brushing out the oil, not just redistributing it on your hair, wrap a piece of cheesecloth around the bristles of your brush or else wipe the brush clean on a turkish towel after every few strokes. Between shampoos, and they might be as often as every three or four days, use cotton pads moistened in astringent to wipe the excess oil off the scalp.

Dry hair will be hard to manage, hard to coax into becoming styles if you do nothing for it. Daily massage will help stimulate the oil glands. Follow it with long, firm brush strokes to distribute the natural oils. In addition, treat yourself to a conditioning treatment when you shampoo. To do it: part your hair off into sections and rub a conditioner (which you can get at most cosmetic counters) directly onto the scalp. When you have covered every inch, wrap your head in a steaming towel and leave it on for fifteen minutes. Then either shampoo or rinse your hair, depending on the instructions that come with the conditioner. Between shampoos, try one of the lubricating preparations to make your hair more manageable.

Dandruff is not only unpleasant, but downright embarrassing when it leaves a mantle of flakes on collar and shoulders. These particles of scaling skin may be there because you haven't brushed your hair sufficiently or because you don't rinse as thoroughly as your should.

Some scalps, of course, just flake more than others. In either case, daily massage and brushing and frequent shampoos are your best help. Always massage and brush to loosen and remove flakes before you shampoo, and be sure you rinse, rinse, rinse. There are a number of shampoos and lotions on the market, many of them containing antiseptics, which can be helpful in fighting dandruff, too.

Needless to say, in the case of dandruff, it is particularly important to keep your brush and combs immaculate, and it's just a rule of personal hygiene not to lend them or borrow anyone else's. If faithful attention to this regimen doesn't seem to be helping, you may have a skin condition that should be treated by a doctor.

And now let's see how to make your hair do what you want.

First question: is it fine or coarse? Straight or curly?

Fine hair, unhappily, if usually apt also to be straight hair. The problem most often is how to keep it from looking limp and sparse. The solution is a short, rather full hair style. Almost inevitably, you'll need a soft permanent to give this type of hair some body. If you use a home permanent, you'll find help in choosing and using the best one for your type of hair on page 65. Using a cream rinse after shampooing, and a setting lotion before you make your pin curls, helps fine hair hold a set longer.

Coarse hair, when it's treated properly, can be a joy. It's most important to have it cut and shaped often by an expert (unless you can become expert at this your-

self), and set in fairly head-hugging styles. A cream rinse after shampooing helps cut down on snarls; and large, even pin curls will reward you with a coiffure that holds its shape and doesn't billow out into bushiness.

Straight hair is by no means the cross some girls would have you think. Healthy, shining locks can be straight as strings and often be more becoming than the most artful curls and waves—provided they are shaped becomingly.

So if you want to make the most of your beautiful straight hair, experiment with the length and cut that does most for your face. And congratulate yourself that you never have to bother with pin curl sessions. Shampoo it, dry it and brush it till it gleams—and there you are. If you decide that curls would be more becoming— and to help you decide, turn to page 60—a soft home permanent will give you the body and curlability you need.

Curly hair, you'd think, couldn't possibly be a problem to anyone, but it sometimes is until you learn to man-

age it. If it's very curly and worn too long or allowed
to become too heavy it will have a bushy look. It's most
becoming and manageable when it is trimmed and ta-
pered often, following its natural waves, and worn in a
medium to short style.

To set it successfully, all you need do is (1) see that
your pin curls follow the way your hair naturally falls
when it is wet, (2) use large pin curls to prevent kinki-
ness, and (3) resist the urge to comb out your set until
it is thoroughly dry.

And, finally, no matter what your hair type—whether
it is fine as a baby's, coarse, straight or curly—the important ingredient in coaxing it into its most becoming
appearance is *confidence*.

Don't be afraid of your hair, don't let it defeat you
into believing that only an expert can make it look de-
cent. Experiment with styles, spend a whole afternoon,
if you can, just plain fooling around with it until you
understand what the problems are. After a shampoo,
comb it while it's wet until you see how it wants to fall.
Push in waves with the side of your hand and see
whether they'll stay or whether you're going against the
grain, so to speak.

This is the way really good hairdressers work. They
realize that no two heads are the same and that a successful coiffure must be based on the characteristics of each
person's hair. If you find your hair hopelessly stubborn, a
soft permanent may give it the needed body to be
manageable. But, you'll be amazed at the difference
it can make once you learn to work *with* your hair, not
against it.

▶ *What's the Best Style for You?*

Naturally, I couldn't answer that question for you
sight unseen. But you shouldn't find it too hard to
answer for yourself if you approach the subject scientifically.

Your hairdo, remember, is a frame for your face, so start by determining what it is you are framing—a heart-shape, a perfect oval, a rectangle, a square or a circle. Do you know the trick for doing that? Draw the various outlines on your mirror with a soapy finger, then see into which one your own face fits best. (Remember that almost every face has elements of several types.) Then study these general tips:

Heart   Square   Rectangular   Round

For a heartshape face, choose a style that adds width to the narrowest part—from jawline to chin, but not at the temples.

For a square face, pick a hairdo that softens it and gives a bit of lift at the top. But keep away from added width at the jawline.

For a rectangular face, use tricks that seem to shorten it—soft bangs and width at the cheekbones. Long, straight hair is usually not becoming to this shape.

For a round face, a short hairdo is best, smooth at the sides and with a slight lift at the top.

For an oval face, that fabled "perfect oval," almost any coiffure can be becoming. Experiment until you find the very best of all for you.

Besides framing your face, your hair style can work wonders of camouflage by distracting the eye from imperfect features, once you learn the principle involved. For instance,

With a prominent nose, bring side hair forward to make the distance from nose to hairline seem shorter. To balance nose, add bangs or a soft lift at the top.

With a short nose, keep hair drawn back from the face and off the forehead. A pony-tail (but a neat one, please)

or a cascade of curls pulled up in the back are both becoming.

With a low forehead, try a little trickery with bangs. Start them *back* of the hairline, keep them soft and just long enough to hide the browline.

With a high forehead, try soft bangs to cut its height.

With a receding chin, direct the eye away from it by wearing a hairdo that has some fullness above the ears.

With a prominent chin, bring side hair forward to cover and soften it.

With a short neck, keep hair up and off the neck. Short styles are best. Long hair should be worn up, not allowed to hang.

With eye glasses, keep bangs, if you wear them, soft and feathery. A side part is usually more becoming than one in the center because it helps to add width to the face.

And now, a final word about *style:* always remember that it must be best for *you.* The fact that a certain hairdo is all the rage won't automatically make it becoming. So consider carefully before you leap for the shears. However, don't fall into the conservative error of deciding that there is only *one* becoming way to wear your hair. Experiment often, within the framework of your individual needs. Because change, after all, is what keeps life exciting.

▶ *How to Set Your Favorite Hair Style*

Given hair that has been properly cut and shaped and that has a permanent if it needs one, there is no great magic to setting it becomingly. Learn these basic techniques and practice them until your fingers become so adept you can practically put up your hair without looking.

To make a pin curl, the basis for most hairdos: take a strand of hair, wind it neatly on your finger to the scalp, slip it off and secure it across the center with a clip or bobby pin. *Remember:* make small pin curls for tight setting, larger ones for loose waves. But in either case, the curl must be a neat, smooth circle with the ends of the hair in the center.

To make curls turning forward: turn the curl toward your face when you slip it off your finger, and pin it flat against the scalp.

Forward

To make curls turning back: make the curl in the same way, but turn it back before you pin it.

Backward

To make a wave: turn the first row of pin curls in one direction, the next in the opposite direction.

Wave

To make stand-up pin curls: (or airy bangs, pompadour effects) don't flatten the curl against your scalp when you slip it off your finger. Stand it on its end and slip a pin or clip through it as you would through a ring.

To get the best results: curls must be smooth, neat and the same size and shape as those nearest. You'll learn by trial and error whether you get best results with water or with wave lotion, with very damp or only slightly damp locks. *Tip* for a quickie set: dry hair completely, then dampen with hair spray.

About rollers: Nowadays, rollers come in a wide variety of sizes. If you're aiming for a hair style that has loose waves or soft curls, by all means try them. But don't expect to get a tight curl with a roller. For very short hair or uneven ends, the newest variety of mesh roller with a bristle inside in an absolute boon. The bristles poke out just enough to catch those pesky ends and

'BRISTLE ROLLER

hold them firmly in place till you've slipped a bobby pin through. If you don't use the roller-with-bristle, you should slip a home-permanent end paper over the strand

of hair before you wind it on the roller. The purpose: it protects the ends of the hair, also keeps the strand together and makes it easier to roll.

▶ *About Permanents*

It's no idle boast by the cosmetics manufacturers, I'm sure, that there is a home permanent nowadays for every type of hair. As a matter of fact, there are so many different home permanents on the market that your first problem may be how to choose the right one.

To simplify the situation, take these three factors into account when you are making your choice:

1. *The kind of hair you have.* Is it hard or easy to wave? Permanents, of any type, usually specify the texture of hair they're best suited for. *Tip:* fine hair is usually harder to wave than coarse hair (unless the latter is the really wiry variety). And if you are giving a permanent to very long hair, you'll probably find you can wind it on rods more successfully than in pin curls.

2. *The kind of curl you want*—definite and long-lasting, or soft, to give body more than real curl to the hair? Rod-type permanents usually give the best results if you want the former. Pin curl permanents are ideal for the latter.

3. *Your own skill.* If you are much more adept at winding your hair on rods than you are at making pin curls, or vice-versa, keep that fact in mind.

Once you have chosen the permanent best suited to your particular needs, the game's half won—but only half. Now whether you end up with a crowning glory, a bushy thatch, or the same straight hair you started with depends on you. To make the most of your permanent:

1. *Be sure your hair is in good condition before you start.* If your locks are dried out or fuzzy from previous permanents, postpone this one until faithful brushing, conditioning treatments, trimming have restored them to health.

2. *Be sure your hair is the length and shape you want it.* Trim off, or have trimmed, any split ends before you wave.

3. *Be sure you understand completely every step of the directions before you start*. When the wave lotion is dripping down the back of your neck is no time to wail, "What do I do now?"

4. *Be sure you have assembled everything you'll need before you start*. Instructions on the package will tell you clearly what that is.

5. *Be sure to pick a time for your permanent when you won't be interrupted or have to hurry*. Skimping on time is fatal to the result—and so is skimping on lotion or the care with which you follow the directions. The people who make these permanents have tested them exhaustively. It's only sensible to follow their instructions to the letter.

Most people find it considerably easier to curl another person's hair than to do their own, so you'll probably get better results with less pain and strain if you persuade your best friend to spend one Saturday helping you with your permanent in return for you doing hers the next week.

And now, are you the girl who said, "I can't do a thing with my hair"? Of course not.

4. That Well-Groomed Look

One of the blessings every girl child is born with is that she needn't be a raving beauty to be attractive. A blessing, since basic beauty is something we can't do much about.

What all of us *can* do something about and what *is* vital to being attractive, is our grooming. Other people are much more apt to notice a powdering of dandruff on clothes, sloppy stocking seams or grimy gloves than they are a too-short nose, an uneven hairline or less-than-perfect legs.

I suspect the reason is that everyone knows we can't change the features we were born with—in short, they're not our fault. But carelessness, sloppiness, untidiness darn well are our fault. They suggest we don't care enough about others to be bothered by the impression we make on them.

A number of things go into grooming, but none of them are difficult things to do. The first step is to become aware of the grooming essentials; the second is to practice them until they become as automatic and effortless a part of life as jumping out of bed in the morning.

▶ *Cleanliness Is Part of Grooming*

Ever notice how grumpy people can get when they want to be clean and circumstances won't let them? The desire for cleanliness is a natural human instinct, and a daily bath is balm to the spirit just as much as it is to the skin.

But there are baths and baths. A six-year-old boy can sit in one for half an hour and come out very nearly as grimy as he went in. His secret: he spends that half hour washing his boat instead of himself, or experimenting with interesting new ways to get water on the floor.

Naturally, we're not so absent-minded about washing as he is, but we are apt to forget about the things we can't see (but other people always can) or the things we think other people won't see. To wit: neck, ears, shoulders and back, feet, elbows. A long-handled brush for shoulders and back, a nail brush for feet, hands and elbows are necessary equipment and should be used daily.

It's surprising, too, how some people will take the trouble to keep themselves immaculate, completely overlooking the fact that their underwear, stockings, gloves, collars and cuffs, not to mention hairbrush, comb and powderpuff, are part of them, too. And if they aren't equally immaculate, the whole effect is destroyed.

Just as tooth-brushing and make-up-removing is part of going to bed every night, rinsing out stockings and underwear should be too. Shampooing your brush and comb when you shampoo your hair is only plain common sense, of course. And don't ever lull yourself into thinking you can "get by" with those faintly grimy gloves or collars one more day. Surer than shooting that will be the day an unexpected meeting or date comes up—and catches you with your best foot definitely not forward.

▶ Daintiness Is Part of Grooming

Unhappily, it's possible to be just as much of a bath-hound as the next girl, and still not be completely dainty. This isn't always so, but it does happen to some of us.

There are, you must remember, roughly three million sweat glands in the human body and for reasons that are beyond me—and maybe beyond science too—the waste products they throw off can be almost odorless in one case, or noticeably unpleasant in another. That's where deodorants and anti-perspirants come in.

To define our terms first, a deodorant simply controls odor; it does not curb perspiration itself. But unless you perspire very profusely under the arms, it should do the trick—used daily, of course. If excessive perspiration, as well as odor, is a problem, try a deodorant-antiperspirant combination. Both types come in various forms—creams, liquids, lotions, etc.—and the label will tell you which is which. Dress shields are a boon, too, to the girl who perspires profusely, helping to protect blouses and dresses from both staining and clinging odor.

Perhaps you're sure you'd never offend. Believe me, it doesn't pay to be smug. Many of us don't, under ordinary circumstances. But given a hot room, a too-tight dress or a sudden access of nervousness, no one but a small child (whose sweat glands haven't yet started to function on an adult level) is safe. Here's where an ounce of prevention really pays off.

There's another aspect of feminine daintiness that needn't pose any great problem once you know how to cope with it—and that is what to do during your menstrual period. Probably you are so conscious of what is going on that you're sure everyone around you must be too, but if you take a few routine precautions, that need never be the csae.

Most important to remember is that, contrary to the old wives' tale, it will do you no harm to bathe or shower daily during your period. The water shouldn't be boiling hot, because that might increase the flow abnormally, or icy cold, which might stop it—but then most people aren't addicted to boiling baths or icy showers anyway. It's especially important not to skip your daily bath or shower at this time for two reasons: there may be some unpleasant odor from the flow itself, and, for some complex biological reason, perspiration odors seem more noticeable then.

It's important, too, to change your napkin often during the day, and always before you go to bed and when you get up in the morning. There are also special deodorant powders to sprinkle on your napkin, and you might find them worth investigating. Incidentally, the word on using tampons seems to be: it can be done, but most doctors feel it's wiser to wait until the menstrual cycle has had several years to settle down into regularity. So, if you're determined to try them, do check with your family doctor first.

For many of us, the menstrual period seems to bring with it the grumbles and the dismals, the hair gone suddenly limp and the skin that's suddenly blotchy. Glands, glands, glands are behind it all, and there's nothing you can do about them.

But you can help the grumbles and the dismals, as well as that skin and hair, by paying extra attention to your grooming *and* your health. You especially need sleep at this time, so make sure you get it (that doesn't mean goldbricking in bed all day, though). Don't indulge in a food binge unless you enjoy courting skin eruptions and constipation. Do wash and set your hair if it needs it (perfectly okay, old fables to the contrary), and take just an extra minute or two to dab on a bit of cologne. Aslo make sure your make-up is just so and your stocking seams straight.

While we're on the subject of daintiness, let's face it: it's always a shock to the beholder to see a clump of hair under an upraised arm or five o'clock shadow on an otherwise feminine leg. In my book, carelessness about these items is inexcusable, and has been since the invention of the razor. De-fuzzing legs and underarms should be done at least once a week—probably oftener in summer. Shaving does *not*—I know 'cause I've checked —make hair grow back faster or thicker. It's probably the simplest and most inexpensive method, though there are others, such as depilatories and wax removal treatments. One tip: if you *do* use a razor, make it your own; brothers and fathers are just plain unreasonable about having their precious razors fall into female hands. Unlike a safety razor, an electric shaver, incidentally, needs no lather.

▶ *For Prettier Hands and Feet*

You may or may not be a girl who "talks with her hands." But whether you are or not, you may be sure your hands will talk for you. There is just no way to keep hands from being seen except by sitting on them or keeping them swathed in gloves. So, clearly, the trick is to make them be noticed admiringly.

Attractive hands are those that are clean, smooth and have well-cared-for nails. That's not too hard to accomplish, is it? Just means regular washing (with a nail brush for nails and knuckles) followed by *thorough* drying, pushing back of the cuticle with your towel, and a quick smoothing on of hand cream or lotion. In winter especially it is almost impossible to keep your hands from becoming rough and red without a hand cream, so make it a point to keep a bottle or tube handy to the kitchen sink and in your locker at school, as well as beside your bed. It also helps eliminate the rough cuticles so tempting—and so fatal—to pick at. A minute of attention to your nails each day, plus a weekly manicure, will keep them in perfect trim. With a little practice you can give yourself a completely professional manicure. Here's the technique:

1. Assemble everything you'll need: a small basin of soapy water, nail brush, orange stick, pumice stone, towel—plus emery boards, cuticle oil, cotton balls, hand lotion, nail scissors, polish remover, polish. and sealer. Just in case your favorite aunt should ask what you'd like for your next birthday, you might keep a manicure kit in mind. It will make it so much easier to keep the things you need together neatly.

2. Take off your old polish with a cotton ball soaked in polish remover.

3. Shape your nails with the emery board. *Tip:* if you're plagued with breaking nails it may be because you file them too far on the sides. Never saw into the sides; shape into an oval by filing towards the center, then bevel the edges.

4. Soak your hands for at least three minutes in soapy water; go over knuckles and nails with a brush and use the pumice (wet) to smooth away any rough spots or calluses. Clean under your nails with the orange stick, but don't *dig* at them. A metal file is not recommended for cleaning because it scratches the underside of the nail, leaving crevices for dirt to lodge in. Dry your hands thoroughly.

5. Cuticles come next. Smooth cuticle oil on each finger and push cuticles back *gently* with an orange stick.

Never cut cuticles unless you have a hangnail or a rough edge. The reason: you're apt to gouge yourself painfully and you're simply laying the groundwork for more hangnails. If these are a problem, the best treatment is to remember each time you dry your hands to push the cuticle back gently with your towel, then smooth hand cream over them.

6. Dip your hands in the water again, go over nails with the brush, dry thoroughly and smooth on hand lotion.

7. And now for your polish. Before you put it on, wipe your nails with remover to take off any traces of oil or cream. Then put on a base coat. Let it dry thoroughly and follow it with two coats of polish. When they are completely dry, apply a coat of sealer—and you've done it just like a pro.

The real secret of a manicure that lasts is allowing the polish to dry thoroughly, so plan this routine for whenever you can have at least half an hour of uninterrupted time. If you do it before you go to bed at night, your polish will have an even better chance to dry and harden thoroughly.

Color tips: your polish should harmonize with your lipstick, of course, as well as with your costume. The darker shades or extreme shades will call attention to your hands, so be sure that's what you want to do before you paint. Shades of red with a bit of blue in them make hands look whiter; the rosy shades or those with an orange cast are flattering to tanned hands.

Incidentally, if you have been a nail biter, you'll find that wearing polish and treating yourself to a weekly manicure is the finest incentive there is to giving up that unsightly habit. It may take a little time to get your nails back into condition, but if you keep up faithfully with your care you'll soon be rewarded with such handsome nails that you wouldn't dream of nibbling at them.

If your nails split and break maddeningly—and not because of your filing technique—make a quick review of your diet. Firm, strong nails call for a high protein diet, that is, one which includes plenty of meat, eggs, cheese and poultry. If you need more help, try dissolving an envelope of unflavored gelatin in your fruit juice or a glass of water every day. It's not at all unpleasant to drink, and though doctors say they don't know *why* it works, it *has* helped scores of women plagued by brittle nails. Allow at least three months, though, for results.

There are special nail hardeners on the market which may help. These are liquids in which you immerse your fingers for a few minutes each day. Buffing your nails daily—which is a good idea in any case because it improves the circulation under the nail—is also definitely worth trying if you want stronger nails. It also will give them such a pretty, soft lustre that you'll have no reason to feel naked without your nail polish.

While we're on the subject of digits, are your toes and feet as well-kept as your hands? Feet are an important part of grooming too, and though they may be on view for only a few months of the year, it takes year-round care to keep them presentable. The first essential is properly-fitting shoes, for the damage that the wrong shoes can do may be irreparable. If you're on a clothes budget, I beg that you do your economizing on

some other item of your wardrobe—not on your shoes. Not, of course, that expensiveness guarantees a proper fit and comfort. Your own common sense tells you that four-inch heels or needle-sharp toes or a size too

small because it's more flattering is bound to reap you a
crop of misery from corns or calluses or misshapen
toes. Unmistakable clue to a flaw in fit: a red, rubbed
spot anywhere on your foot. Don't ignore the warning.
It's a forerunner of a corn.

Your feet deserve, and welcome, a thorough scrubbing
each day, so don't forget them when you take your bath.
Keep a pumice stone handy to smoothe away pump
bumps and calluses on the sole (but *never* undertake to
cut or shave them.) Wield your orange stick, then, too,
to keep cuticles from running wild. Be sure to dry your
feet thoroughly, specially between toes, and sprinkle a
little dusting powder on them before you slip on stockings. Or, if pump bumps and calluses are a real problem,
rub them daily with hand lotion or cream. For if these
accumulations of dead skin are allowed to become
hard and dry they're much more difficult to cope with.

To dress up your feet for summer sandals or the beach,
treat them to a pedicure. The technique is the same as
for a manicure, with one important exception: never
cut toenails down on the sides. They should be cut
straight across, level with the tip of your toe, then
smoothed at corners with an emery board. To neglect
this rule is to court ingrown toenails—very painful
things to have. When you put polish on your toes,
you'll have less trouble with smears if you use rolls of
cotton to separate each toe until the polish has dried
thoroughly.

▶ *Fragrance—and How to Use It*

Perfume is the final touch in grooming, adding a
subtle but positive dimension to your personality. Women
have known the powers of fragrance since Cleopatra's
day, when the ladies of her court anointed themselves
with sweet-smelling oils.

For many years only the very rich could afford the
precious little bottles of scent that worked such magic,

but today surrounding yourself with a pretty scent is no longer a wild extravagance or a dreamed-of luxury. Toilet water, colognes, scented bath powders, sachets are in everyone's reach. But there still remains some art in using them to the utmost.

So, let's take a quick lesson in that art.

Perfume is the most highly concentrated form of fragrance, which is why it smells stronger, lasts longer—and costs more. There are a number of different perfume families—the floral scents, the spicy scents, the oriental scents, and so on. There is no one family which is particularly suited to a particular type—blonde or brunette, for instance—so make your choice on the basis of your own preference.

But do follow these rules when you shop for perfume: don't sniff directly from the bottle; the scent will be too strong really to savor. Instead, ask the salesgirl to dab a bit on the inside of your wrist, let it dry a minute and then sniff. And don't try to sample too many fragrances at one time. Your poor little nose will get completely bewildered.

Toilet water and cologne come in the same scents as perfumes but the fragrance is much less concentrated because more alcohol and some water have been added to the essential oils. Since their price is usually a fraction of perfume's, and their scent weaker, you can use them more lavishly. But don't expect them to last so long on your skin.

To make the most of your precious perfume, remember these commandments:

1. Use it on the pulse spots—the inside of your wrists, your temples, the crook of your arm, along your throat. The blood is close to the skin's surface here and its warmth helps keep the perfume's fragrance alive. Perfume dabbed behind the ears, incidentally, is perfume lost. No one, including you, will be able to smell it.

2. Never put perfume directly on your clothes. It may leave a stain that will never come out. And if you put

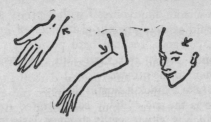

perfume on your throat, make sure it's dry before you add pearls.

3. Don't experiment with making your own scent by mixing odds and ends from different bottles together. Even Petunia would be ashamed of the results you'll get.

4. Don't hoard your perfume. An opened bottle will keep its fragrance intact for only a few months, so use it up while it's still sweet. Tip: that's why it's smart to buy it in small amounts.

5. Don't expect the perfume you sprayed on before the dance to last all evening. Carry a purse flagon with you for touch-ups later.

There are many delightful ways to use fragrance. Why not add one of these to your repertoire?

• Spray your closet with a *light* cologne.

• Don't throw away empty perfume bottles. Tuck them into your underwear drawer to give your lingerie a light fragrance.

• Put a few drops of perfume on a bit of cotton and tuck it inside your bra.

• Pour a little toilet water or cologne into the final rinse water when you're sudsing undies. Makes them smell yummy.

• Don't think you can't enjoy bath oil because you're a shower addict. Smooth a little on your body before you step into the shower. Its scent will cling pleasantly.

• When you shampoo your hair, spare a drop or two of perfume for the rinse water.

▶ *Quick Cures for Calamities*

They happen to all of us—the run in a stocking as you set out for a party, the unexpected date that finds you with stringy hair, the blemish that pops out the day of a dance. They can ruin your evening if you let them. But a smart girl doesn't. She's learned what to do and has the materials to do it with when calamity threatens.

A blemish on your pretty face spells disaster, you think. It needn't. Resist the urge to squeeze it and camouflage it instead. Use a medicated lotion, cover it with a tinted

make-up stick that blends with your skin tone. Or use a medicated lotion that has tint in it. The trick is to match the color of your own skin and to smooth your camouflage on carefully so that no one can see where it blends in. Frequent blemishes, of course, mean all is not well with the inner you and it's time to take a critical look at your diet.

If an important occasion catches you with eyes reddened and swollen from weeping, don't despair. Cold packs, promptly applied, plus eye drops, will restore them to normal very quickly.

It never seems to fail that when you are planning to wash your hair tomorrow, it's today that divine boy you just met asks you out. There isn't time, of course, for a real shampoo and set—but there is help at hand. To remove some of the oil that makes it look so stringy, use the trick of a piece of cheesecloth on your hairbrush, backed up by a hundred firm strokes. Then part your hair into sections and gently clean your scalp with a piece of cotton moistened with witch hazel. Now for the set: use hair spray for setting lotion, make pin curls as tight as possible. Let them dry—about ten minutes—comb out and spray again. Who'd have believed such a major repair could be done so fast and successfully?

Is it your cross that when you get nervous your hands get damp? Very distressing, I know, when hand-holding is a possibility. The solution: cross your palms, not with silver, but with an anti-perspirant before you set out on that date.

Do you find that the worst part of a cold is the chapped red nose and upper lip that inevitably follow? They certainly make it hard to look or feel attractive if you let them go untreated. So use hand lotion to soothe and smooth the irritated area, then tone down its fiery looks with tinted foundation and powder.

Shadows under the eyes are likely to mean you've been living it up just a bit too much and not getting the sleep you need. Resolve to do better on that score, but meantime use a make-up stick to cover those droopy shadows.

"Nothing to wear" is a familiar wail, which of course

can be translated as "nothing *new* to wear." If you have to make an old dress do duty once again, take time to put it into fighting trim. Make sure it's spot free, press it with a steam iron, and see what a different scarf, a flower, a belt or a pin can do to change its personality.

A broken fingernail sticks out like a sore thumb—especially when the others are perfect curves. If the nail has broken off completely, a falsie pasted on and painted the same color as the others will hide the damage till the nail has grown out. If the nail is simply cracked, you can save it, for the day, at least. Put on a coat of colorless polish; while it's wet press a small piece of tissue paper over it. Cut the paper to the shape of your nail and cover it with several coats of polish. Clear adhesive tape does the same job well, too.

It's nice to have an electric personality, but electric hair full of flyaway locks can be a nuisance. Here's a simple way to tame it: brush it into place, then dampen the palms of your hands and smooth them gently over your hair.

A fever sore, let's face it, is something of a calamity no matter when it happens. But you can make your mouth feel more comfortable and look more presentable while it is healing. If you get fever sores often, it's worth investing in this equipment: a drying solution like campho-phenique, plus a hypoallergenic lipstick in a pale shade (less obvious) which won't be irritating. If you use the cream, put lipstick over it. *Tip:* you'll get a much clearer outline if you use a lipbrush.

Well, enough talk of calamities. Now that you know how to cope with them, let's move on to more cheerful topics and talk about that vital matter—clothes. But don't leave grooming behind. It should be part of you always.

5. You and Your Wardrobe

▶ The Well-Dressed Woman's Secrets

Nothing gives a girl more self-confidence than knowing she's well-dressed, and nothing makes her feel more miserable and *un*-confident than the suspicion that her clothes are unbecoming or unsuitable.

Some girls, I'll grant, seem to have an inborn "flair for clothes." They instinctively know how to pick the color or contrive just the effect that will be most becoming and distinctive. But they are few and far between. And there's no reason why their more numerous sisters, once they have absorbed the know-how, shouldn't achieve just as successful effects. Let's take a look at what makes a well-dressed woman.

If you had a chance for a leisurely peek into the closet of a woman famous for her chic, you would probably notice, with some surprise, that none of her clothes are examples of the latest fad—unless it happened to be a fad or fashion that seemed to have been made for her. For the basic secret of a clothes sense is knowing, or learning, what is becoming.

"But that's what's so hard," I can hear you wailing. It's not, though, if you approach the matter scientifically. If you'll make a mental review of your wardrobe and single out the dress or suit you wear over and over again from the failures that always get pushed to the back of the closet you'll find that your favorites:

—suit your coloring
—suit your figure
—suit your type

These are the three keys to a flattering costume, so the first step to a successful choice is learning to analyze yourself.

You've probably known since you were fairly young that there is one particular color that makes you look sallow or washed-out, some other shade that always seems to give your looks and your spirits a lift. Those are the two extremes, but there are dozens of in-betweens that will fall on the plus or the minus side as far as you're concerned. Before you buy another stitch, find out what they are, so you'll have your own personal color chart in mind next time you shop.

Experiment, without investing a penny in failures, by holding lengths of fabric up in front of you. The ones you chalk down on the plus side are those that are keyed to your skin, your hair, your eyes. If your own coloring is delicate, the softer more delicate shades will enhance it, while extreme, dramatic colors will make it seem mousey. But if you are the girl of raven locks and dead white skin, or brilliant eyes and rosy cheeks, or flaming tresses and pearly complexion, you can carry off the more dramatic shades successfully. If your blue eyes are your proudest possession, you'll find that a blue scarf or hat or dress seems to make them even bluer. If you have a pink-and-white complexion, the rosy shades will make it seem even more peaches-and-cream. Try out lots of colors, and when you find the ones that suit you, stick to them.

By now, there's nothing you don't know about your own figure—or there shouldn't be, unless you've been playing ostrich. You know whether you're tall or short, thin or plump. Of course, if you're neither tall nor short, but just in between, not thin, not plump but a perfect size 12, you're incredibly lucky and you'll look fine in anything from a bikini to a sheath. Otherwise, you must keep your figure firmly in mind when you shop and never talk yourself into believing that because the dress looks adorable on the hanger it will necessarily do so on you.

Knowing what your "type" is may be a little harder. The best way to find out is to experiment within a basic framework, using "soft and feminine" as one end of the scale, "casual, tailored" as the other. Working from that point, you'll find yourself almost unconsciously developing tricks of dress to enhance your particular type and give it individuality. A word of caution, though: don't aim to be the "sophisticated" type unless your face and figure are flawless.

The second secret of the well-dressed woman is knowing what to wear when and where. This can be a puzzler when you're just starting out as your own authority on your wardrobe. After a while, experience and intuition cue you so that the chances of finding yourself all wrong for the occasion are practically nil. Meanwhile, the safest rule to follow is: it's far, far better to be underdressed than overdressed.

If what you have on is basically simple, good, neat, and worn with confidence, it can never be really wrong.

Of course, it's only common sense to find out ahead of time what's planned for a date or what the other girls are wearing to a party so that you don't turn up for a hayride in high heels or for a party in Bermudas where everyone else is in formals.

But please, please, please don't let conformity become a fetish. It's one thing, and a good thing, to wear the right clothes for the occasion. It's another thing, and often a disastrous thing, to wear a style just because everyone else does. The number of girls who fell for "the sack" and were real sad sacks in it is ample proof of that point.

Our well-dressed woman has a few other tricks up her sleeve, and they're good ones to learn. What makes her stand out, besides the basic becomingness of her clothes, is often some tiny detail—a particular accessory, the way she knots a scarf at the neck of a sweater, the way she places a pin, a spark of color in just the right place. These are tricks, ways of attracting or fooling the eye, and she has learned them the way you will have to—by using her imagination and powers of observation, by experimenting and taking the time to figure out that "special touch" that becomes a trademark.

Just as one small detail can *make* an effect, it can break it. Shoes that don't go with a purse, the wrong color gloves, a white collar with a spot on it can ruin the most carefully thought-out costume. That's why women who are really expert at dressing themselves wouldn't dream of going to a party or an important event without dress-rehearsing everything they're going to wear—trying on dress *with* shoes and all the other accessories—not only to make sure they all look well together but also to be certain a ripped seam, or a stain, or shoes that need shining won't face them at the last minute.

▶ *Putting Together a Wardrobe*

The old problem of a closet full of clothes but nothing to wear is a familiar one to every woman at some time or other. If it's yours, take steps right now.

The first one is to make a complete inventory of what you own. List the contents of your closet and bureau as "good," "possible" and "hopeless."

If there's nothing to be done to improve "hopeless," get rid of it *now* No one enjoys the reproach of a failure staring her in the eye every time she opens the closet door or bureau drawer.

"Possible" probably means that dress would be fine if you ever got around to shortening it, or you never wear that blouse because it's lost a button. So stop and do what's necessary to move all the "possibles" over to the "good" list.

Now you know what you've got to work with. And you're ready to see what you need. Because the really workable wardrobe is one that's planned *before* you go shopping.

While you have that pencil and paper handy, make a list of the activities and occasions in your life; under these headings put the clothes items you already have, so you'll know the gaps you have to fill. Then—and all-important—figure out what you can spend on filling the gaps and how to apportion the dollars.

Then etch on your brain this maxim: *The successful wardrobe is one that is becoming, useful, within my budget.*

Now, you know what you need, you know what you can spend, you know what's becoming to you, so it's time to go shopping. And I'm ready to give you a whole slew of tips before you set forth. They are:

1. Remember that good, basic, simple styles will have nine times as many lives as extreme or fussy ones.

2. Don't be detoured into buying a sequin-spangled sweater when you set out to get—and only have enough money for—another school skirt.

3. Never let yourself be lured into buying a dress or suit that's going to entail a whole new set of accessories—unless money is no object.

4. Remember that mix-and-match separates are a dandy way to stretch a small wardrobe.

5. Know your size. Once you find out whether "teen," "junior" or "misses" sizes are best suited to your proportions you'll have fewer disappointments and fewer bills for alterations.

6. Remember your shopping manners, and your shopping sense. By that I mean: explain clearly to the sales-girl what you're looking for. If you despise polka dots or frills or sleeveless dresses it will save wear and tear on

her temper and yours if she knows that from the beginning. Don't try on clothes you have no intention of buying, just to while away the time. This isn't fair to the salesgirl who could otherwise be waiting on a customer who wasn't fooling. When you do try on something, it's only common decency to be careful you don't rip it or smear lipstick on it or leave it in a crumpled heap on the dressing room floor. And, finally, don't buy it unless you're absolutely *sure* it is what you want. The dress or sweater or blouse you hope will look better when you try it on at home rarely does.

▶ Choosing a Suit or Coat

In any wardrobe a suit or a coat usually represents the biggest investment, and a failure in this line is hard to shrug off. So, if you have been hoarding your clothes allowance for either of these items, here are some points to keep in mind when you take the plunge:

1. Unless you're already lucky enough to have several coats for different kinds of occasions, your wisest choice is one in a solid, neutral color. Both pattern and color can limit its wearability enormously. For example, gray or beige will go with almost anything in a wardrobe, and so, surprisingly, will red if it's a clear, true red without too much of either orange or blue in it.

Don't, however, fall in love with a gray or beige or any other color that is so pale and fragile that it shows every spot and smudge. If you do, the coat will spend most of its life at the cleaners.

2. If you are buying a winter coat, try to keep a realistic picture of your climate in mind, even if you're trying it on at a spring sale. If winters are cold where you live, steer clear of coats that have no collars, have loose sleeves or are clutch-type instead of buttoned in front. It will be a very shivery winter indeed if you don't.

3. I don't care how mad you are for it, if either a coat or a suit is going to need major alterations to fit you, it will never live up to your expectations. Any honest tailor would give you the same advice, believe me.

4. To make sure either garment is going to be really practical and useful, try the new coat on, before you buy it, over whatever suits you own, and try on any contemplated suit under your existing coat. If they won't work with what's already in your wardrobe, their usefulness will be pretty limited.

5. Finally, since you will be spending a good deal of money, presumably for quality, make sure the quality is there and that you aren't being taken in simply by a pretty color or new silhouette. Suits and coats are meant to last for several seasons, so make sure the fabric has the staying power for it. If it's very soft, loosely woven or just plain sleazy between your fingers, it won't.

You can check the workmanship by giving a careful inspection to: the lining (shoddy linings are a big giveaway), the seams (they should be ample and well-finished), the stitching (smooth and uniform is what you're after), the buttonholes (which should be cut on the grain of the fabric, neatly and firmly finished so they won't sag or rip), bindings (neat!) and buttons (to make sure they're firmly attached with a long shank).

If a coat or suit fails all these tests, I personally would back quickly away from it. If it fulfills all the requirements I've mentioned, you really have a buy!

▶ *How to Choose Accessories*

Under the heading of accessories I would list as essential: hats, shoes, gloves, purses, scarves and belts. Other items like mad mittens or shocking pink leotards are fun to own, but they're likely to turn up under the Christmas tree or beside the birthday cake, so what *you* have to concentrate on is the basics.

I have learned from bitter experience that the wise shopper and smart dresser—one and the same girl—owns *fewer* but *better* accessories. It is very *un*canny buying indeed to invest in a belt or purse just because it's inexpensive and you might find something to wear it with some day. Though accessories are small items in your wardrobe, they can make a big difference in it and they should be plotted and planned for with as much care as your spring formal.

When you buy a hat, be sure it will go with the coat and suit you have, as well as with several of your dresses, that it's becoming and that you feel comfortable

in it. Don't let the salesgirl sweet-talk you into something that makes you feel foolish once you get it home. (Not that I'm against an occasional mad, crazy hat—provided your face and budget can afford it. It can do wonders for morale.)

Shoes that torture your feet in the store will torture them when you get them home. So unless you haven't a nerve in your body or a brain in your pretty head you won't waste your money on ones that aren't well made and well fitted to your foot. I feel so strongly on this point that I think every woman should some time have to see the plaster casts foot doctors have made of feet horribly deformed by badly fitted shoes. The next things to consider are color and material. Off-beat colors that go with only one thing you own and fragile leathers or fabrics are strictly luxury items.

A purse is usually chosen to go with shoes you already have, so that takes care of color. One word of caution: consider its inside shape as well as its outside shape before you plunge. Its contours may look awfully smart but may make it almost impossible to find anyting in—and it soon winds up at the back of the shelf.

A good leather belt lasts and lasts—my favorite is fifteen years old. Of course, it must be becoming to your figure (very wide or brightly colored belts are not for short girls or hippy girls) and well made. If it is both it will give new looks and new lives to dresses and skirts year after year.

For penny-watchers, I think the most important consideration about gloves is cost of upkeep. Certain suede, kid, doeskin gloves will have to go to the cleaner when they're soiled; fabric gloves—and these are getting bet-

NO   YES

ter every day—can go right into the basin and be ready to wear next day.

Scarves are to have fun with. Forget about cost, for-

get about durability. Pick them with color—and you'll
find marvelous ranges of shades—and for a fabric that
you can do graceful things with. The scarf that's old
faithful in your wardrobe might have cost fifty-nine cents
or five dollars.

So, finally, keep in mind: one carefully chosen accessory is worth five ill-considered ones—not only in dollars
but in sense!

▶ How's Your Seamsmanship?

If you love pretty clothes—and who doesn't?—learning to make your own is about the smartest thing you can
do. Dressmaking is an art that loads of fashion models
practice, for not one but for several good reasons. For
anyone who's asking for them, here they are:

1. $$$$ and more $$$$—though there are other important reasons. Seriously, though, almost everyone
knows that you can make two or three dresses for the
price of one you buy.

2. Starting from scratch with a dress or skirt or blouse
is the best way I know to learn what's your type and
what becomes you. You start with color and fabric
and proceed to style and fit, discovering as you go along
what's for you an what isn't in each category. Besides
that, you have the fun of creating—combining and adapt-
ing patterns, developing styles that are completely yours
and yours alone.

3. If you've wasted hours shopping fruitlessly for a
particular blouse or jacket to go with a skirt you have, or
for a color that's vivid in your mind, you know how frus-
trating your failure can be. The girl who can just "run it
up" never faces this frustration.

4. If you've ever spent any time in the yard-goods department of a store, you've probably noticed that the
fabrics you see in bolts come in a wider variety of
quality and color than those that make up ready-to-wear
clothes. And since it takes only three or four yards to

make a dress, they're not beyond your budget by any means. Learning about fabrics is a wonderful way to develop an eye for color and a flair for fashion, and you can't help but learn about them if you make your own clothes.

So, my advice is: get in there and sew, girl! If there isn't a sewing machine in the family, see what you can do about borrowing or renting (the latter is usually not costly), or investigate the second-hand machines. Your mother, your own clothes sense and the dozens of how-to books and booklets available should soon put you on the road to happy fashion sewing.

▶ *Fashion Tricks That Fool the Eye*

Whether you buy or make your clothes, here's an even dozen tricks for making sure they're most becoming:

1. One-piece dresses and up-and-down stripes make you look taller.

2. Two-piece outfits, especially if they're in contrasting colors, make you look shorter.

3. Wide belts and belts that contrast with dresses, cut height.

4. A V-neckline makes face and neck appear longer.

5. An off-shoulder neckline adds width to the figure.

6. A round or square neckline makes face seem rounder.

7. Stripes and plaids attract the eye more than solid colors. Horizontal strips and plaids cut on-the-straight add width to the figure.

8. Princess lines are slimming.

9. Black, in large amounts, absorbs color from the skin, can make pale coloring look washed out.

10. White reflects color and is becoming to all complexions but the very sallow.

11. Large collars broaden the shoulders and shorten the figure.

12. Too many colors worn together create a fussy, distracting effect.

▶ *How Much Jewelry?*

Too much jewelry is much worse than none at all—a comforting thought for the budget-minded. Probably you have some already, so if you are thinking of splurging on a new piece, review your present supply, just as you did your wardrobe, so that you'll be sure of filling a gap, not duplicating what you already have.

Almost certainly you'll want a few classic pieces—a strand or several strands of imitation pearls, a pair of pearl earrings, and quite possibly a gold bracelet, with or without charms. Then fill in with a few additions each season to add color and variety to basic costumes. If you buy inexpensive items you can afford to follow gay new fads without worrying too much about whether they'll be out of fashion next year.

▶ *Protect Your Investment*

To end this chapter on fashion know-how on a purely practical note, I'll remind you that the way to get the utmost out of your clothes money is to buy good things and take good care of them. What happens to your clothes when you're *not* wearing them has just as much to do with how long they'll last as what happens to them while they're on you.

Can you look your closet in the eye? Is everything hung up neatly on wooden, plastic or padded hangers, with fastenings closed and shoulders in place? How about bureau drawers? Are they a jumble of slips with broken straps, sweaters with spots on them, stockings with runs in them? If they are, today is the day to straighten them up. Tip: dividers, stocking boxes and cases for gloves and scarves are a great help in keeping drawers tidy and the contents thereof in the neatest shape.

Taking a moment to brush woolens, velvets and corduroys before you hang them up at night is sound economy two ways. It not only lengthens their life but lengthens the time between expensive trips to the cleaners.

And, while we're on the subject of cleaning, experience has no doubt already taught you it's much easier to get a stain out if you attack it right away—and with the proper tools.

To help on that score, many cleaning establishments have free booklets on home stain removal—very useful information to have since the prevalence of synthetic fibers and blends in modern fashions has made many of Grandma's cleaning maxims obsolete.

If home treatment of stains fails, or clothes are just plain all over dirty, it's penny-wise-pound-foolish to put off sending them to the cleaner. Ingrained grime eats

at the fibers and shortens the life of clothes. If you're sending something with a stubborn stain on it, pin a note to the cleaner pointing out the spot and what you think made it. It's much more likely to come home minus spot. And never, never press a garment that has a stain you haven't removed. You'll "set" it so that even the cleaner may not be able to remove it.

If you make it a rule to polish your shoes and handbag before you put them away, you'll be rewarded by having them all gleaming and ready on the morning you oversleep or the occasion you have only ten minutes to get ready for. Besides keeping them looking spick and span, polish protects the leather and lengthens its life enormously.

The dread clothes moth has probably already taught you that out-of-season woolens must be put away *clean*. Sprays and garment bags won't protect them if they're not, and when next winter rolls around your beloved cashmere may look more like a lace bedjacket.

Since I've given you so much work, I'll save you a little with this hint: since cotton and linen dresses inevitably have to be pressed when they come out of hibernation in the garment bag, you save yourself doing the same job twice by putting them away rough dry. And with wool or crepe dresses you can often spare yourself a stint at the ironing board by using the old bathroom steam trick.

Run the water hot in tub or shower, close doors and windows, and let the garment hang near the steam (but not near enough to be sprinkled) for half an hour. Presto, it's pressed.

So far we've talked about health, beauty and clothes—how to wear them and how to care for them. In short, we've covered the externals. So, now let's move on to the Inner You.

Part 2

The People in Your Life

6. The Boys in Your Life

► As a Group

Probably what seems to be the most crucial problem in your life right now is boys—how to meet them, how to attract them, how to handle them. It needn't be a problem, but it will undoubtedly remain an interest long after the girls have turned into women and the boys have become men, so it's a subject well worth studying up on now.

I think the best tactical approach to the subject of boys is to take them, first, as a group, and second, as individuals. I say this because whether you're interested in meeting them or in being popular with them, the group is what you have to contend with first.

The herd instinct is strong in the American male, as stagline attitudes prove only too clearly. Boys tend to do things together, to stick together, and to accept or reject together. The true lone wolf is a rare animal. Although there is no reason in the world that you, all by yourself, shouldn't strike up an acquaintance with an awfully nice

boy who is all by himself, the law of averages says you
won't. It's much more probable that you will run into
him with a bunch of his friends. And if you want to
make a specially good impression on *him*, you have to
make the grade with *them*.

Believe it or not, there really is nothing very mysterious about the qualities in a girl that makes boys like
her. All they need is a sporting chance. Because actually,
behind the kidding or the studied indifference, boys are
every bit as anxious as girls to be popular with the opposite sex. But since social custom has always given them
the upper hand by making them traditionally the
choosers not the chosen, they can conceal the fact more
easily.

Perhaps this is what makes them so critical of the
girl who can't conceal her yen for popularity—who either
goes overboard in her eagerness to attract male attention,
or, at the other extreme, loudly voices the sour grapes
view of "Boys—phooey!"

If she takes the first course they feel she's pursuing
them; if she takes the second she's insulting their
masculine pride. That's why I'm convinced that honesty
—to a point—is the best policy with boys. If you assume
a pose, it's very likely to be seen through and laughed
at, or, if it isn't, it scares them off.

If you've ever taken the time to do any reflecting about
which girls are popular and which aren't—and why—
you have undoubtedly noticed that one characteristic
popular girls have in common is the ability to be relaxed around boys. They are frank, but never frantic, in
their attitude that men are wonderful creatures. They
make no bones about enjoying their company, but
they never give the impression that they consider the
hours spent *out* of their company so much wasted time.

How did they ever achieve this enviably relaxed point
of view, you wonder? Probably partly by exposure; perhaps they have been lucky enough to have brothers and
brothers' pals to hang around with since the sandpail

days. Men haven't suddenly appeared on their horizon like a blinding light. These girls also have a certain maturity of perspective that tells them boys aren't the be-all and end-all of life. They're wonderful—but so is a sunny day in May.

Now, why does the simple fact that a girl is relaxed around boys make her popular? Easy. Because it makes *them* feel comfortable. They don't have to fend her off on one hand or knock themselves out in an effort to impress her on the other. They feel she likes them as people, not as acquisitions, and they make it clear they like her by beating a path to her front proch.

It sounds as easy as 1-2-3 on paper, but I realize full well it's no simple trick to seem relaxed if you don't feel it. However, there's only one way to do it and that is to try, and keep trying until one day you find you feel as easy in the company of boys as you do sitting at your own dinner table.

Here is where a special skill or hobby or interest can be your ace in the hole. Boys, you've noticed, are usually doing something, and if it's something you can do too, you not only have an entrée into their group but you have a reason for being in it, and you automatically feel more relaxed. So it's a smart girl who doesn't spend so much of her time working out a knock-'em-dead outfit or restyling her hair that she never learns to be a good swimmer or a keen skater or a champion in the bowling alley.

Besides being clannish, boys are basically conservative, especially when they're together. Have to keep up the side and all that, you know. They may whistle at the girl in the low cut red dress, but it's the demure little one in blue they ask for a date. The girl who shrieks or whose laugh can be heard around the block, the one whose clothes look as if they came straight out of her mother's closet or whose make-up is by Technicolor does not make the grade with the group for long, if at all.

Besides being clannish and conservative, these maddening males are also keen-eyed as hawks. If you don't believe me, listen to these gripes aired by a group of college freshmen. Asked what they considered the most dire female crimes in looks and dress, they unhesitatingly came up with:

- Make-up so heavy it comes off on a boy's jacket at a dance.
- Eye make-up that's so extreme a girl looks like a Chinese vase instead of a girl!
- Smeary lipstick. It's disgusting to see it all over coffee cups and napkins.
- Fingernails that belong on the bride of Fu Manchu.
- Dresses that look as though they'd been painted on.
- Dresses with necklines that end slightly above the waist.
- Dresses that may be right in style but aren't becoming.

• A get-up that would look great at Buckingham Palace—when the date's informal.

• Not knowing the difference between casual and rumpled. (Ouch! That one really hurt.)

• Charm bracelets that clank so they drown out conversation.

• Jewelry so blinding a guy needs dark glasses.

• A raucous voice or sloppy speech.

• Stance like a football player's in a huddle.

• *Sloppiness!* And this was echoed with such shaming particulars as:

• Chipped nail polish

• Underwear straps that show

• Wrinkled stockings

• Unshaven legs

• Grubby handkerchiefs

• Stains on dresses

• Unsightly feet

I guess that makes it pretty clear that boys don't miss a trick when it comes to a girl's appearance. So never let that look of sleepy indifference lull you into carelessness about the impression you make. Besides making it very clear what boys object to, this awesome list can show you what boys like. Read it again, and a picture of the girl whose appearance they admire should also be clear. She is neat, she is sweet, she is clean, and perhaps most important, she is *understated* (to borrow that favorite fashion word), not only in her dress but in her make-up, her accessories and her manner.

This same group of boys waxed even more vocal on the subject of behavior—particularly date behavior. But we'll take that up in a little while. Meanwhile, a quick review of the rules on boys as a group: To meet a boy, look for a group; have a reason to be in it; friendly and attractive to all the boys, not just the one who takes your fancy, or you'll soon find yourself voted out.

▶ *On a Date*

So far as I know, there are no hard and fast rules about
the age at which dating begins, or, for that matter, about
what constitutes a date. It might be any activity shared
with the opposite sex—from a couple going to the movies
to a dozen couples going on a hayride. The basic fact
that makes a date different and, oh, so exciting is that
he asked *you* to be his partner. So you want to be sure
that everything goes perfectly from beginning to end.

The beginning, to be strictly accurate, is when he
asks you for the date. The way you accept—or refuse, if
you must or want to—will have a lot of bearing on
whether he asks you again. Or whether anyone else
does, for that matter. Boys gossip too, you know.

No matter whether you're so thrilled by the invite
you're sure he must hear your heart pounding, or about
as excited as you would be at the prospect of an evening
with Frankenstein, remember that ordinary rules of
courtesy and either accept quickly and enthusiastically
or regret quickly and regretfully. It may well have taken
some doing for him to screw up his courage to ask you,
so if you give him any more reason for feeling uncomfortable he'll be sorry he ever did.

Two pet peeves boys have on this subject are the girl
who tries to stall—"I'll let you know Thursday" or "I'll
have to see"—in case a better bid should come along in
the meanwhile. Also the girl who won't accept a date
until she knows what the date is for, making it clear that
the pleasure of having the boy's company is not her primary interest.

This doesn't mean, of course, that if you have to ask
your parents whether you may go out or whether you
may go to a certain place you shouldn't say so frankly.
Any boy who is worth going out with will respect that
reason for not giving him an immediate answer, but he
will be quick to spot and resent any less valid one.

Naturally, once the date is made, you must not break it unless you have an equally valid reason. Girls who break dates just because they feel like it or because they think it looks sophisticated or because a better offer came along soon have no dates to break.

When D-hour finally arrives, please, please be ready! This plea has been voiced so loudly and repeatedly by men that perhaps I don't even need to mention it. But in case you're either a sufferer from chronic lateness or just can't resist building up the suspense a few minutes longer, consider how you like sitting in a strange living room being closely inspected by someone's little brother or quizzed about school by someone's father. An evening that starts this way is going to have a hard time getting off the ground.

Whereas, if you are at the door to greet your date, looking your prettiest and most welcoming, if you introduce him to your family as though you're really pleased that such wonderful people have a chance to meet each other, if you have a few phrases of introduction ready such as, "Dick is on the school paper with me" or "Tom is crazy about old cars" to help him start a brief conversation with your parents, you'll have made a warm place for yourself in his heart before the date has even begun!

Now all you have to do to keep up the good work is to keep on being considerate of your date—and his wallet. If he's made plans for the evening don't try to change them, no matter how much you hanker to see the double feature at the Palace or to show off your beau to the gang at the Pizzateria. Boys resent bitterly, and they have every right to, the idea that they're being manipulated or pushed around on a date. It reduces them to the status of a means of conveyance.

The only grounds for not following a boy's plans for the evening are if he suggests going to some place your parents have not given you permission to go or if he suggests some sport or activity you don't know how to do. In either case, tell him frankly what the situation is: "Gosh, I'm sorry, but I'm not allowed to go there. Could we take in a movie instead?" or "Before we go I'd better tell you I've never bowled before in my life—but I'm game if you are." This honest approach will leave both of you feeling much less awkward than you would feel after some lame or farfetched excuse.

Being considerate is also one of the secrets of a successful conversationalist—and conversation is often the biggest pitfall of a first date. Some people can't think of anything to say—so they don't. Result: date soon becomes tongue-tied himself.

Others can't think of anything to say so they fill the silence by gabbling incessantly, mostly about themselves. Result: date's eyes are soon glazed with boredom.

Some think that talking about all the other boys who admire them is an impressive topic of conversation. Result: date makes a mental note to let the other boys have them next time.

If panic strikes, and you find yourself veering toward any of these dire alternatives—Stop! Get a grip on yourself. Remember that it's easy to talk about the things you're interested in and one of the things you're interested in is your date—or you wouldn't be out with him. So start with him—what he likes, what he doesn't like, what he does with his spare time, what he's planning for his future. The conversation will soon be rolling along smoothly as a Cadillac on a super highway. If your interest in him is genuine, no man can resist it long.

If you haven't kept him waiting, haven't changed his plans, the talk is going smoothly and you're obviously having a good time, the date is almost bound to be a success for both of you.

But there is one other pitfall I should mention, and that is doing, saying or wearing anything that makes your date feel uncomfortably conspicuous. As I said before, men are conservative creatures. They are also sensitive souls with invisible antennae that can pick up for miles any disapproving glances or comments on their date's behavior. It's terribly important to them to be proud of the girl they are with—so be sure they can be proud of you.

▶ *The Girl They Don't Ask Again*

Remember I mentioned that that group of college freshmen had also said a mouthful on the subject of girls and dating? Want to hear who it is that they wouldn't ask out twice? Be brave, I hope you're not on the list:

"The girl who makes my pockets sag with all her

make-up equipment because she's too lazy to carry a purse."

"The babe who orders the most expensive dish on the menu—and then doesn't eat it."

"The girl who thinks it's *so* gay to take off her shoes at a formal dance."

"The one who makes it clear that anything I can do she can do better."

"The gal who thinks she has to smoke to be sophisticated—and then bums cigarettes from me all evening."

"The girl who wants to be sure everyone knows I'm her date—and sees that they do by keeping a stranglehold on me all evening."

"Any gal who corrects me in public. She might get away with it once, but never twice."

"The date who ignores my friends or gravitates to her own the minute we get to a party, leaving me out in the cold."

"The prima donna who always likes to face a mirror so she can admire herself while I'm talking to her."

"The make-up artist who spends more of the evening in the ladies room repairing her face than she does with me. And why is it they always go in pairs?"

"The girl who leaves 'thank-you' out of her vocabulary!"

And that's the word from your severest critics! See if you can't make those critics eat their words.

► *Perfect End of a Perfect Date*

Inevitably, the date has to end, and inevitably you must say goodnight. How smoothly you manage your farewells may decide whether you'll be called on to make them again.

In the first place, make sure you're not the girl who's dropped "thank you" out of her vocabulary. If you had a marvelous time, and you probably did, don't leave him guessing. There's nothing square about being sincere and vocal in your appreciation. Don't forget that all the time you were worrying about whether you were making a good impression on *him*, he was worrying about the impression he was making on you. If he knows that you had a good time, he has nothing to worry about.

That fabled goodnight kiss is the next topic that's likely to arise. And it's a topic that calls for tactful handling. If you don't feel like kissing a boy goodnight, there is no reason at all that you should. A kiss is not the price of a date.

But if you're a smart girl you'll have thought out your strategy ahead of time so you'll be able to dodge the issue adroitly and spare your date's feelings instead of being forced to duck abruptly and leave him with his pride badly lacerated. While you and he are sitting in that darkened movie house you have plenty of time to decide whether he is the type who will probably try for a goodnight kiss—and also whether you like him enough to bestow it. If the decision goes against him, take another few minutes to figure out how you're going to play the game your way. If your family is still up when you get home, you might ask your date in and say goodnight in full view of Mom and Dad. If they're not, you'll just have to be sure you have your thank-you's and good-night's all said before you reach the door—and then don't linger.

And don't lose heart if your technique isn't smooth as silk the first couple of dates. Unless a girl is downright rude, boys are pretty philosophic about a refusal.

7. The Girls in Your Life

▶ Why They're Important

If you stop to think about it, you'll realize that girls are even more important in your life right now than boys are. They are the ones you share your secrets and your plans with, they're the ones you learn from. And they're the ones you spend most of your time with. You may have lots of boy friends, but I doubt if any of them is a friend in the way that another girl can be.

It's a wonderful feeling to have a "best friend." And, if you want to have any social life, lots of girl friends are a practical necessity. Girls, not boys, are the prime movers in parties and group activities, and it's usually through other girls that you meet new people and develop new interests.

▶ Making Friends

It's not hard to do; in fact, it's so easy once you know how to go about it that it's better not to be in too much of a rush to claim someone as your best friend. Try to be pleasant to all the girls—even the ones you secretly think are "stuck-up" or "dopey"—for you never know what a person is really like until you really know them. And when you find a girl or several girls who seem to like the same things you do, who have the same interests you have, show them that you'd like to be their special friend.

Don't be too shy to make the first move—the other girl may be shy too, and then what have you? A deadlock. A friendly overture, a sincere compliment, a casual invitation is rarely rejected. So make an excuse to walk home from school with some girl you'd like to know better. Or tell her you think her sweater is a glorious color, if you do. Or ask her if she'd like to come over to your house to hear the new record you just got.

Asking someone's help is another good way to make friends with her, and sometimes seems the easiest way if you're shy. Everyone loves to feel she can do something especially well and can't help being flattered if you ask her to show you how she does it—whether it's setting her own hair, making her own clothes, doing a dance step or writing wonderful book reports. First thing you know you're practically living at each other's houses, and your families are complaining because no one else ever gets a chance to use the phone.

▶ *To Keep a Friend*

It takes two to tango, remember, and it also takes two to keep a friendship going. It will wither as fast as a rose out of water if one friend is always the giver and the other always the receiver. If Suzy expects you to help her with her algebra regularly, she should be prepared to heed your wail for help when it's time for another home permanent. I don't mean that either of you should keep a running score on the favors done for the other— that would be more like a business than a friendship. What I do mean is that reciprocity is the foundation of friendship.

A friend who isn't dependable is a thorn in the flesh. If Jane says she'll meet you at the tennis court at eleven sharp, and slopes around at 12:30, if she promises faithfully to come over after supper and help you pin up hems, then never shows up, your patience will soon wear thin. Besides the natural irritation of being stood up we're also likely to feel that people who break dates or promises, who keep us waiting or who rearrange our schedules to suit their convenience can't really care as much about us as they claim to. My response is to give them up after a while and find another friend.

Loyalty, of course, is an absolute must in friendship, and one of its greatest comforts. When you've just broken up with Bill, or your mother has bawled you out about the state of your room, or your little sister has become absolutely unbearable, whom do you turn to? Your best friend.

You know you can count on her to listen to your woes, to take your side, to help you out of a jam if she can. If there's one of those sudden reshuffles of the group and you find yourself temporarily out in the cold, you've still got a friend—if she really is a friend.

No matter how great the temptation, deserting a friend because of group pressure is absolutely taboo. So is catting. People have lots of high-flown alibis for being catty: "telling her for her own good," or "being objective about her faults," or "it was so funny, I just couldn't resist telling about it." But they don't fool anyone, and they do wreck a friendship fast.

Boys can make or break a friendship between girls. If you want to be sure it's not the latter, remember the rule: "Hands off the other girl's beau."

Probably the greatest pitfall in a friendship is jealousy and possessiveness. And the closer the friendship the greater the danger is. If you and another girl have been spending practically every waking hour together, if you know every last little detail there is to know about each other, if you have confided things to each other that no one else in the world knows, it's only natural to feel some resentment when a third party barges into your beautiful relationship. It's almost impossible not to feel jealous because your friend now has someone besides you to confide in. But if you show your jealousy by being possessive or spiteful you only create an ugly situation which is bound to leave you unhappy, bitter and minus just a little of your self-respect.

My advice is to try and remember that *all* relationships have to change eventually, even those of the most happily married couples. Try to accept the inevitable with as much grace as you can. If you don't try to hang onto your friend with the blind stubbornness of a three-year-old hanging onto his toy truck in the playground, you may still keep her as a friend. Not so intimate a one, granted, but perhaps in another few weeks you'll have a new best friend yourself.

▶ *When Friendships Break Up*

Of the dozens of friends you've had so far, and the dozens more you'll have, probably not more than one or two will remain lifetime friends. This isn't because one or the other of you has failed in loyalty or generosity or reliability. Changing groups, changing interests, distance, or any number of other things may make you drift apart. It may seem too bad, but it usually isn't too painful—just one of the facts of life.

And that's the way to look at the break-up that isn't gradual or caused by distance. It's a fact of life, too, that the person who seemed closest to you last week may be practically a stranger next week. The world is moving fast—and so are you. For months the biggest interest in your life may have been tennis or modern jazz or fashion drawing. Suddenly it bores you stiff and what you're all hopped up about is shell collecting. And so, Alice, who used to seem to you the most fascinating, glamorous creature you'd ever known, suddenly seems just like all the other girls, and you can't find much to say to each other.

If this happens, neither of you should feel upset or disloyal or betrayed. If you both handle the break-up gracefully, your interests may touch again some later day—and you'll be back living in each other's pockets. If not, you'll at least remain friendly acquaintances and not bitter enemies.

8. In the Group

"Hey, come on, the gang's going over to the roller skating rink!"

The words are music when you're one of the gang. But if you hear them addressed to someone else while you're walking home from school alone, they can make you feel dreadfully lonely and left out.

We all feel the need to be part of a group at some time, and we probably feel it most when we're young. Sometimes it happens automatically—you've gone around with the same bunch since third grade and never had to give the matter a thought. But sometimes you have to devote a little thought and effort to belonging.

▶ *If You're New in Town*

When you move into a new community and start in at a new school everyone but you seems to be busy,

busy, busy. Exciting things seem to be happening in everyone's life but yours. "Who needs me?" you wonder wistfully. "Who has time to be bothered with me?"

The answer is that almost any of these busy people do, if you show them that you're there.

The easiest and most obvious place to make new friends, of course, is in school. But just sharing a classroom with a dozen or more people your own age doesn't necessarily guarantee your becoming a social sensation overnight.

If you want to be "in on things," you have to go out for things. If you're good at any sport, waste no time in getting on the school team. If sports honestly bore you stiff, investigate the other extra-curricular activities—the school newspaper or yearbook, the debating society, the glee club, the dramatic club, the science clubs. Don't be like the artist who starves in his garret while he waits for his paintings to be "discovered." Try out!

See what's going on at your church. It's not just a place to go on Sundays, you know. In most churches there are young adults' groups or fellowship groups with regular weekly social programs, lectures, even trips. Ask what they are and how you may join.

Summer time is probably the easiest time to meet new people—provided you don't spend it moping in your own back yard. Stroll over to the lake or the public pool or the tennis courts. You don't need an engraved invitation to get in on the fun at these places. If the public recreation spots are too far away for you to get to on your own, you'll probably find it isn't hard to lure the family into a Saturday outing in the car.

And don't overlook the various community organizations in your town and what they can offer in the way of fun and friends. The YWCA's Tri-Hi-Y groups is one example; 4-H clubs, Girl Scouts, Campfire Girls, Girls' State are others.

Besides these, in almost any community there is always a volunteer job to be had for the asking—working for a charity, a fund drive, settlement house, hospital or Sunday school. "But who would I meet in those places?" you're probably asking. The answer is: You never know, and that's what makes life exciting. New friends pop up in the most unexpected places once you start to get around. But you'll never find them by sitting at home!

▶ Meeting People Halfway

Before you rush to cast your lot with any group, make the most of the advantage that being a temporary outsider gives you. Unlike the gal who belongs to a group simply because she grew up with it, you have the opportunity to look around and choose your friends.

Choose those you'll have something in common with. Don't be in such a hurry to lose yourself in a gang that you forget that the lasting friendships and the really good times are with people who share your interests. And this, incidentally, is the time to broaden your interests, to learn the skills or take up the hobbies you've always thought might interest you.

Whether "the group" is an organized one that you sign up with or just five or six girls in your class who always go around together, if you want to be accepted as one of them the first few moves most likely will be up to you. They're not hard moves to make.

If you have a smile and a friendly word for everyone, if you show that you're interested in whatever it is they're doing it, it won't be long before you're part of the inner circle. Needless to say, if the gang bowls every Thursday or takes a hike every weekend, and you're a champion bowler or a hiker from way back, it's duck soup. But even if you're not, don't despair. Willingness to learn is a most appealing quality.

Actually, your own attitude probably has most to do with how quickly you can make a place for yourself in any group. If you feel shy, the best thing to do is admit it frankly. All of us are shy in certain situations, and so we're more than glad to try to make things easier for someone else who is obviously suffering through the same feeling. But most people are not part-time psychiatrists; they're not going to realize that aggressiveness or haughtiness or touchiness are disguises for shyness.

Don't make life unnecessarily hard for yourself by deciding that a group, thanks just to sheer force of numbers, is necessarily unapproachable or unfriendly. People are still people, whether they're singular or plural, and a group is rarely a charmed circle that you may not enter. Unlike the small, tight (and in my opinion, rather unattractive) cliques whose main purpose seems to be excluding more people than they include, the average gang of boys and girls in a school or community is a relaxed and friendly bunch, willing to make room for any new member who promises to be an addition.

Your parents can be a big help when you're trying to break the ice in a new community. Don't misunderstand; I don't mean that Mother and Dad should behave like a pair of social directors at a dude ranch—they'd probably

be as horrified by that idea as you would; but if you
know that you can ask a new acquaintance to drop by
on the way home from school and be sure of finding a
welcoming smile and some cold drinks in the refrigerator,
it's a great help. And don't overlook your mother as
a possible gold mine of ideas on the whole subject of
making new friends. She went through it all herself,
you know.

What all of this really adds up to is: if you remember that the group you want to belong to is a collection
of people you'd like to be friends with, and not a for-
tress with a moat around it, the battle is half won.

Unless you're the world's greatest gift to something or
other, don't sit at home waiting for new friends to come
and find you. But don't, at the other extreme, let your
eagerness make you try to "push" your way into a
group. Here's where the old rule of meeting people
halfway really applies.

And, finally, remember that one surefire way *not* to
be popular with any group, as many a girl has learned
to her sorrow, is to lay siege to one member and ignore
the others. The one who is sought out may be momentarily
flattered, but the rest of the gang will be resentful of what
seems like an attempt to break up existing friendships,

and the newcomer will soon find that the majority has voted her right straight out!

► *Must You Follow the Leader?*

One of the comforts of being part of a group is the reassurance it gives to do things that other people are doing, to think the way they think. Often we're not sure exactly how to behave in a new situation or what attitude we ought to take about a new idea. If we're on our own, we have to take a chance and hope we're right. But if we're part of a group, we can always look first to see how the others are doing things. If we do as everyone else does, we don't have to run the risk of looking foolish or ignorant or calling forth disapproval.

Playing it safe this way is fine, when it's a simple question of when to sit down or stand up or how to get an oversize shrimp into your mouth gracefully. But it can be treacherous when it lulls people into just blindly following the leader or the crowd. Because the crowd is not necessarily always right.

You've read about, and probably seen, mobs and gangs. Both of them are examples of what happens when individuals decide that the face of being a group gives them the right to do things they'd be afraid or ashamed to do by themselves.

It's not easy and it's not fun to be a dissenting minority of one in a group whose good opinion means a lot to you. But your own good opinion of yourself will mean a great deal more. All our lives we are faced with choices and decisions that no one else can make for us. If we try to evade them, or agree with the majority opinion just because we're afraid our own opinion will be unpopular, we're cheating ourselves more than anyone else.

If your group takes a stand or plans an action that you think is stupid or cruel or dangerous, or just silly, stand up and say so. You needn't start a battle royal if you don't want there to be one. Simply saying, "Sorry, but I can't go along with that one," is your right, as it is every individual's. And don't worry too much about the disapproval. If it comes, you'll still know you're right, and the chances are that when they think about it, most of the other members of the group will know it too.

9. For a Happy Home

This chapter might be called "Trouble in Paradise." It's on a subject that is touchy, important, and impossible to ignore: your relationship with your family. It's very likely that things don't seem to be the way they used to be between you and your parents, and perhaps they don't seem to you to be just right.

If you were a normally lucky child, until quite recently you probably didn't think much about your parents; you just accepted them the way you accept the warmth of the sun on a lovely day. You feel the sun, but you don't often look up and reflect on where all that light and warmth is coming from. It's too familiar. And so are your parents. True enough, there have been cloudy days, even stormy days between you three, but always the sun came out and life went back to its normal pattern.

Until now.

Well, what *is* happening now? The details vary, but it could be any number of things on the order of:

"My mother nags me so much."

"My father is so sarcastic about everything."

"Mother criticizes every single thing I do, but she's

always sweet with my younger sister, who can do no wrong."

"Mother criticizes *me*, but is very sweet to my older sister, who can do no wrong. My older sister can wear lipstick, spend hours on the phone, go to the movies practically every night, and Mother doesn't say a word. But if I try to do any of those things she gets furious."

"My parents want to know every single thing I do. I think I have a right to some privacy."

"My father is suddenly laying down the law about everything. Mother used to be the one who made the rules, but he's taken to issuing orders right and left."

"My parents don't like my friends. They don't realize that these kids are very popular, and anyway they're *my* friends. Do they want me to go around all alone?"

"My parents expect me to do more than any human can do—get A plus in school, do housework and errands, be in bed by nine every night. When do they expect me to have any fun?"

And finally, though it's hardest of all to admit, "They just don't seem to like me any more—not the way they used to."

The complicated thing about all this is that the girl who made one or more of the complaints I've listed would probably be right—and at the same time dead wrong! We'll get back to that paradox in a minute, but first let's see if the list of troubles is complete. Unfortunately we may not be quite finished counting the thistles that have suddenly bloomed in the garden of family life.

All we've mentioned so far are the things your parents do that you resent or find unfair. What about the things you do, or, even more important, the feelings you may have—feelings you don't really think about but which may account for behavior that suddenly and unexpectedly makes trouble? They're not feelings a girl would be proud of or ever want to utter, but if she did, some of them might be:

"I used to have so much fun with my father, but now he kind of bores me."

"Why can't my mother run our house as well as Mary's mother runs theirs?"

"My parents don't seem to have a single interest outside of the house. They never do anything new or think about anything new. They don't seem to care about what's going on in the world."

"Sometimes Mother or Dad try to kiss me or hug me as if I were still a baby. It's awfully embarrassing."

"Why are they always trying to find out what I'm thinking about? Isn't that my business?"

"Sometimes I wish I could just get away by myself and not have to be supervised all the time."

"My mother is awfully dumb about some things. She just doesn't seem to get the point."

"When I have a fight with my parents about something, they act like such bullies I just hate them. I wish they didn't get me so mad."

That's enough. By now, you've surely got the point. The details of each person's life are unique; the fundamentals of all lives are the same. Among the most important of these fundamentals are parents, and often a person wishes this weren't the case. Sometimes the troubles between herself and her parents are so painful she wishes there were no such thing—and at the same time she loves them dearly, more than any other two people in the world.

While you have sense enough to know that no one's parents are perfect, you can't help feeling that everyone else's are. You're critical of your parents and resent their being critical of you. You're disappointed in them, and ashamed of being so. No wonder you're confused.

Don't be. It's not so complicated as it seems. Nine times out of ten it all comes out in the wash. Relax, don't take it so hard, and let's see what this problem of hurt and misunderstanding between parents and teen-age daughters is all about.

The first thing it is all about is love. That may seem surprising because most of us think of love as romantic love—boy and girl, man and woman, the sort of love that is a fulfillment of dreams, that shapes a life.

One might think that the love between parents and their children is a totally different thing, that it should more properly be called affection. After all, there's nothing romantic about it; it doesn't involve falling in love, or choosing the person to love, and it is something that often isn't expressed much. Neither parents nor children think about it, in fact. It is just there, taken for granted. But in spite of all this it is still love. It is a fact of life, an instinct, and, whether parent or child knows it or not, one of the strongest they will ever experience.

A family is not just a practical arrangement by which a girl lives with her parents and is looked after by them until she's old enough to go off on her own; it's a real emotional relationship between individuals, each of whom means a great deal to the other.

There are two physical laws of nature, which, oddly enough, also apply to our emotions. One is that for every action, there is a reaction, an opposite force. The other is that nothing in the world remains the same; everything changes, sometimes so slowly you can't see it, like the weathering of rocks; sometimes as rapidly as the tumbling of a wave.

Emotionally, the law of action and reaction means that the more you love a person the more disappointed you are when he does something you don't like. Disappointment, when it is strong enough, makes a person feel hate. Boiled down, this means: the more you love someone the more you hate them when you're mad at them.

The law of change means that no matter how serene, how much in balance your relationship with anyone may be, time changes each of you. The change in one is felt by the other, who must adjust to it in turn, and so it goes. Probably neither of you is actually aware of it while it's happening, but it does happen all the time to you and everyone you know. With your friends, as I've mentioned, unless there's some special bond to hold you together, the changes gradually cause you to drift apart.

These changes take place, too, in the relations between parents and children. But unlike the situation between friends, families have a great deal to hold them together. Neither parents nor child can say, when the going gets rough, "Well, so long. It's been nice knowing you," and go their separate ways. They have to struggle through this new situation, in spite of quarrels and misunderstandings. Usually in a couple of years they come out on the other side, so to speak, and find that once more they are good and loving friends.

There will be a difference in this new relationship. Young adults can view their parents' faults with a clear eye and forgive them easily; parents of independent young adults can view their children's independence without resentment or worry. And at the same time each can feel underneath this new relationship which seems more like a friendship, the deep bond that began to be forged years earlier, when the child was born.

That's the ideal, and that's the way life works out a good part of the time. Sometimes, of course, it doesn't work out. Sometimes young people and their parents have such a hard time during this period of changing adjustment that the minute the child can get free he grabs his independence and runs. We all know men and women who left home as early as they could and never came back. When that happens it is too bad. Both sides will always feel they are missing something they could have had.

You, of course, are a long way from anything like that. I only mention it to point out what your goal is in relation to your parents and your treatment of each other now. It's simple: You want to grow up and become an adult independent of your parents, which means you want to change your relationship with them, but change it without wrecking it.

What makes it seem hard is that the relationship you're trying to change began a long time ago. When you were a small child, your parents were all-powerful, and they were all you had. If you thought about them at all, you probably assumed they'd been put on earth for the express purpose of protecting you, feeding you, clothing you, putting up with you and loving you. That's how you saw them, and, more important, that's how they saw themselves. Each of you formed a habit of feeling toward the other, and it's a habit you can't break suddenly, the way you might give up chocolate or stop wearing a pony-tail. It will only change slowly, as circumstances force it to change.

Are you wondering what all this has to do with the real and specific complaints that began this discussion? How does it help you to handle them? What good is all this talk, when you and your parents are in a deadlock, when you and your mother are glaring at each other over the breakfast table, or your father has just announced that you certainly may not go out with Jim tonight? I hope it will help by giving you an idea of what is really going on between you, and by showing you that solving the problems really is worthwhile.

That's what I meant some pages back when I said that in your complaints you are both right and dead wrong. You're right that these troubles do exist; you're wrong if you think they mean that you and your parents don't love each other and can never get along.

So—what to do about it? Try compromise. Like peace, it's wonderful!

Take the question of nagging or criticism, for instance. Probably your parents do nag and criticize you more than they used to. The more obedient and loving you were as a child, the more surprised and hurt they may be now when you aren't so loving and obedient. Probably the more dependent on them you were as a child, the more strongly you feel now about trying things your own way.

The best solution is: stop fighting so hard. Remember the law of action and reaction. The harder you pull in one direction, the harder they'll pull in the other. Don't give your parents so many occasions to nag you; try to do things their way once in a while. It won't kill you. It is usually little things—conflicts over such issues as keeping your room neat, or helping with the dishes, or getting your homework done—that bring to the surface the violent emotions on both sides that are really caused by your growing independence.

"My father is so sarcastic," was one of the complaints I mentioned earlier. That's very possible. This is a man's standard response to something he doesn't understand, and since when have men understood women? A father is, after all, a man and not a god. A teen-age girl is closer to being a woman than to being a child.

You're not the sweet, obedient little girl who used to think everything your father did was marvelous. You're baffling to him, and he isn't sure whether or not you're going to turn into the kind of woman he likes. But he doesn't want to come at you head on or jump on you when he can't quite put his finger on what's wrong. So he snipes at you. Don't worry about it too much; he doesn't really disapprove of you so much as you think.

And what about your father suddenly laying down the law? When you were little, he left your care to your mother because that struck him as woman's work. Now you're beginning to move into the adult world, a world he feels he knows something about. He's worried about these important first steps you're taking and he wants to make sure that the big decisions are the right ones. It didn't matter much to your father whether or not you ate your applesauce when you were six. It matters a great deal to him whether you go out with what he considers the right kind of boy.

"My parents don't understand me; they don't understand how the other kids in my group think, why it's so important to me to do certain things"—and so on. This is all true, perhaps. But how *could* your parents understand you. They're not mind readers. They don't know what goes on at your school, in your social life, and, most important, in your head. I grant it would be almost impossible to tell them—tell them all of it, that is.

But they weren't born yesterday, either. Try to tell them a few things, at least to give them some clues as to why you feel strongly about certain things. You can be factual, you don't have to go into details if you don't feel like it, you needn't "tell all," but you can still give them an idea of what's going on in your life so that it won't seem to them that your insistence on some point is utterly irrational.

This brings up the important point of privacy. You want it, and you're right to want it. But remember, to your parents this is something new, too.

When you were small, you may have thought your feelings were hidden at times, but usually you were transparent as a glass of water. And, too, you enjoyed confiding in them, and they liked your doing it. Now, when you act the sphinx, it's a rebuff to them. You are, in effect, telling them it's none of their business, and this hurts their feelings and worries them as well.

They want to know what you're thinking and feeling because they care about whether life is going well for you or not. So try to give them a break. Keep to yourself what you feel you must, but give out as much as you can. And when you do refuse to discuss some things, try to make it clear that you're doing it, not because you don't love them or don't trust them, but just because some things are impossible to explain.

One of your instinctive reasons for wanting privacy,

by the way, is so that you can make your own decisions without interference; another is fear that your parents will disapprove. The first is a pretty good reason, but the second is not. They probably won't disapprove so much as you fear. If they do, the chances are that they are quite right to, and that what is going on is something risky or unwise.

Finally, we come to that rather tricky point on the list —the feeling that your parents don't seem to like you as much as they used to, and that if you have a younger or older sister, their treatment of her seems to emphasize the point. Probably, if you're honest with yourself, you'll admit that this feeling of yours just is not founded on fact. Your parents love you as much as ever; they just find it hard to express it when the old hugging-kissing relationship is gone, and at the same time you seem so unfriendly yourself. Meanwhile, your little sister is still their sweet little baby, and your older sister has fought her way through to a new basis as a grown-up daughter.

As for all the troublesome feelings about parents that we listed earlier in this chapter, they can be quite easily summed up as the result of starting to view two human beings as human beings and not as gods. Don't be ashamed of those feelings, they aren't so disloyal as they seem. They are the other side of the coin of your parents' feelings about you. When you get used to seeing your parents as people, you may understand them better. Their flaws and limitations won't bother you because by then you'll have your own life to lead. Nothing that ever happens between you will make you so mad as it does right now, because later your independence won't be at stake every time you disagree.

I began by calling this chapter "Trouble in Paradise." Perhaps I could sum it up now by saying that Paradise never existed, but once you thought it did. Now you're leaving that imaginary place for the real world. It may be a hard transition, but the real world is what you want most of all.

10. Building Your Personality

► **Taking Stock**

At the beginning of this book I suggested you take a long look at yourself in a full-length mirror and make an objective list of what you saw—the features that pleased you and those you thought you could improve on. Wasn't too hard, was it? And once you took the time to see where work was needed, the next steps were obvious.

Trying to look objectively at the parts of you no mirror shows—your mind, attitudes, feelings, talents, behavior, the qualities that all together make up your particular personality—is not so easy, alas. And yet it is something that all of us are continually trying to do. "What kind of person am I really?" is a question that haunts us most of our lives.

When you were a child you were probably too busy finding out about the rest of the world to do more than take yourself for granted. When you're older, the life you lead, your work or career or family, the kinds of things you enjoy and the friends you have, will help to answer the question.

Right now, though, is when knowing the answer seems most vital to you—to your social life and your entire future. And who can supply it? Not your friends—they're trying to find out the same thing for themselves. And your parents aren't sure either because you're not the same person you were yesterday, and they're not clear who you'll be tomorrow. And so you have to come back to yourself for the answer. "Who am I, anyway? What am I really like?" you keep asking.

It's fine to ask, but do please give yourself a break when you answer. Don't magnify your bad qualities and minimize your good ones. Don't decide that because you're not perfect you must be a perfect mess. We'd all like to be perfect, I imagine, but there just ain't no such beast!

So the only constructive course is to try and do the best we can with the self we've got. What we want most is for other people to like us, and for that to happen we have to like ourselves. It's darn hard to be likable when you're tense, anxious every moment about how you're "going over," too absorbed by your own short-comings, actual or imagined, to have any real interest to spare for others.

The popular person's secrets, as I've pointed out before, are simple ones: She is relaxed, and so makes the people around her feel relaxed too; she's genuinely interested in other people and genuinely friendly in her feelings toward them. She doesn't assume poses, because

she's satisfied to be herself (though not so satisfied as to be smug, let me hastily add); and she takes it for granted that other people will be satisfied with her too.

I don't mean to sound, though, as if popularity automatically comes to a person with no effort on her part at all. Just saying, "I like me and I like you, so therefore you'll like me too" is not going to do the trick. There are techniques involved in being popular, and the more they're practiced the easier they become.

The essential technique is learning ways to communicate your interest and friendly feelings to other people. They're not mind readers, after all, and can't be expected to know how you feel till you show them. That's what smiles are for, and friendly greetings, and interested questions, and small acts of thoughtfulness. None of these calls for any special talents and they all get results.

▶ *Overcoming Shyness*

At this point, the obvious stumbling block is shyness. All of us are shy, in varying degrees and different situations, but how many of us ever stop to think about what shyness really is? Basically, it's fear—fear of being snubbed or rejected and fear of not showing up well in a particular situation, or of being made to look a fool. We've all had dozens of fears in our lives and either got over them or arranged our lives so the fear didn't hamper us. If you're afraid of heights you can stay off mountain tops, but unhappily I don't know of any way to arrange your life so that shyness doesn't hamper it—unless being a hermit sounds appealing. So, obviously, it makes sense to work on overcoming it. I know it's not so easy as it sounds, but there are hundreds of important and successful people in public life today who are proof that it can be done.

First step is to stop—right now, this minute—taking it for granted that any group you have to enter is unfriendly or waiting eagerly for you to make a fool of yourself. Tell yourself these strangers think you're great and they're all rooting for you. Chances are, of course, they may not even be aware yet that you're among them, but, when you get right down to it, it is no more conceited to assume everyone thinks you're great than it is to assume everyone despises you—and it's much, much better for morale.

Another reason for feeling shy in a group is the mistaken notion that you have to justify your presence in it (why should you, any more than anyone else?) and you don't feel your conversational powers are up to it. The best trick then is to keep busy. At a party, if you can help the hostess or pass out the soft drinks, you *do* have a reason for being there, and a smile or a pleasant greeting is all you need to take you out of the corner and set you to circulating from guest to guest. It's almost impossible for us to feel foolish or ill at ease when we know we're being useful or helpful. Look for ways to keep yourself busy, no matter what the group you're in.

You'll feel more comfortable in social situations, too, if you take the time to learn the accepted customs—about which more in the next chapter. If you know your manners are always good, that you can count on yourself to know what to do when, it can't help but bolster your confidence.

If you have any particular interest or talent, work on it,

girl! It's next to impossible to remember you're shy when you're talking about a subject that fascinates you (and that you *know* you know a lot about) or when you are doing something you know you do well. If you could sing like an angel or play the piano like Van Cliburn, you could probably be the life of the party without ever uttering a word.

But there are lots of other talents, and much less exacting ones, that can work wonders in smoothing your social path. One of the homeliest girls I ever knew—she looked exactly like a James Thurber dog—was also one of the most popular girls in our crowd, mostly because of the screamingly funny monologues she could do. I might add that she was also the first to get married— to a swooningly handsome and desperately shy young man!

That handsome, shy young man brings me to another point, which is: one of the best ways to forget about your own shyness—and start off equal with the popular girl—is by thinking about how the other person or people you're with feel. Give the other guy credit for sensitive feelings, too, and see what you can do or say to make him feel more comfortable and at ease. If you really concentrate on it, the first thing you know you'll have completely forgotten about yourself.

Finally, here's an experiment I wish you'd try some time soon. Is there a girl in your school or on your black that you've never done more than exchange glances with? Perhaps you decided the very first time you saw her that she looked "snooty," so you've made sure she'd never have a chance to be snooty to *you* by keeping out of her way. Or perhaps you spoke to her once and thought there was a hint of a snub in her expression or answer, so you've never tried again. Well, make that girl your guinea pig. Go out of your way to smile at her, to greet her by name when you see her and show you are interested in her whenever there's an opportunity. If you like, remind yourself that you are doing this deliberately, as an experiment. But just see how long it takes to win that girl over. Not very long, I'd be willing to bet. And if you don't succeed in winning her over, you still have the upper hand, because she's bound to feel increasingly uncomfortable about her rudeness when you are so pleasant, and you'll have the satisfaction of knowing you made every friendly overture possible, instead of the nagging worry that perhaps you hadn't met her half way.

If you like people and learn the ways to show it, they'll find it very hard not to like you.

► *Traits That Worry You*

I don't know why it is that when we have a trait we're not too proud of, we're sure that no one else is guilty of it but us. We fret and stew and tell ourselves accusingly that no one else could waste so much time daydreaming or that no one could possibly be so tactless as we are. And then along comes somebody and makes a survey which shows that practically everyone else worries about the same traits in themselves.

I don't mention this so that you can relax and say,

"Well, I'll stop worrying, then, and go right on being tactless," but simply to point up the fact that you are not alone, ever, in your shortcomings. The people you admire most may have the very same ones, or if not those, some others.

But it does make sense, of course, if you have a habit or trait that you know is a bad one or that's holding you back socially, to see what you can do about overcoming it. Here are six that are most often mentioned by young people as the trait in themselves that worries them particularly: feelings get hurt easily; constant daydreaming; crushes; flightiness or fickleness; tactlessness; gossiping. Let's see what might be done about them.

It's very uncomfortable, I know from bitter experience, to be the girl whose feelings are constantly getting trampled on. A "crack," a look, a reproof, a snub, can make you burst into tears—or want to. Your parents or your friends may tell you you're too sensitive, but that's cold comfort, even when it's kindly meant; or perhaps they say it's "your own fault" for taking things too hard.

Don't fall for that "fault" line; it is not a fault to be sensitive. In fact, sensitivity is one of the greatest gifts we can have, if we know how to make use of it. It's the sensitive person, not the one with a hide like an elephant's, who can most enjoy people and ideas and beauty. But do try to keep your sensitivity from turning you into a defenseless target.

In the first place, don't allow yourself to go looking for trouble—seeing a slight where none was intended. In the second place, learn to get some perspective on the things that others say and do that hurt you. Take the time to try to understand what her motive was, and also to think about whether whatever they said or did is really worth being offended by. Sometimes the unkind things people say or do are so petty that it's easier to feel sorry for them than to be hurt by them. With experience, you'll find that it becomes simpler to gauge which things in life are worth troubling about and which are really not important at all.

Daydreaming is something that everyone does some of the time. As a matter of fact, it's one of the ways we use to try and answer the old "Who am I?" question. Picturing ourselves in a variety of situations, or as we would like to be, is not a complete waste of time, and it is certainly pleasant. but, like lots of other pleasant habits, moderation is the rule with this one, too. If you let yourself daydream most of the time, the first thing you know you'll be out of touch with the world—and even possibly flunked out of school.

If you're worried, or your parents or teachers are, by the amount of time you spend on Cloud Nine, it's time to ask yourself some questions: What is it you're daydreaming about all the time, and why do you think you're doing it? Is it boys? Or clothes? And is it perhaps because you don't know as many boys as you'd like to or haven't many chances to be with boys? Or you're crazy about pretty clothes and haven't as many as you'd like? Or you haven't anyone to talk with about the subjects that interest you most? Well, daydreaming is never going to get you the real thing, and you must admit that the real thing is better than fantasy. So why not spend some of that time and energy on trying to get what you want or be the kind of person you'd like to be instead of just dreaming about it?

Often people daydream purely as a way to escape from the surroundings they're in. If you're snoozing your way through school and find it impossible to keep your mind on what's actually going on in class, there's something wrong with your approach—or the school's. Make an honest effort to see what it is. Are your classes so hard for you that you've given up? So easy that you're bored? Are they dull because of the way they're presented? Talk to your parents about the problem, or talk to the principal or guidance counselor at the school and see if some changes can't be made to improve the situation.

Finally, learn to be firm with yourself. You can break this habit like any other, or at least keep it in comfortable control, once you make up your mind to. If you feel yourself floating off on Cloud Nine when you should be down to earth, don't just float. Hop off.

"Crushes" come in a number of varieties, and they're basically a perfectly normal phenomenon. We've all had a crush, some time: on another girl, an older woman, and countless boys and men. They're really steps along the way to learning how to love another human being on an adult level. Babies and very small children don't know how to love anyone but themselves; they have to learn gradually to love those around them.

When you have a crush on a girl your own age or slightly older, you're drawn to her because at the moment she seems to be everything you'd like to be; in another six months she may not seem that at all. When you have a crush on some older woman, it probably has something

to do with that war for independence you're waging at home. You no longer want to be that worshipful little girl who thinks everything Mommy does is perfect, and yet you can't help missing just a little having someone to worship. So you pick someone outside the family, possibly even someone as different as possible from your own mother. For a while, she seems to you the wisest, most wonderful woman in the world. In a few months or a year she'll resume her normal shape in your eyes and be just another person—a nice person, most likely, but no more extraordinary than any other.

Crushes on boys come and go so fast you can hardly count them, and may be prompted by things as seemingly illogical or unimportant as the sound of his voice or the way he quirks his eyebrow. One of my deepest crushes, I remember, was on a boy I saw exactly three times. The first time I encountered him he gave me a ride on the back of his bike—and I was hooked. The second time, mad with love for him as I believed I was, I snapped his picture with my Brownie camera and promptly hung it on a locket around my neck. The third time I ran into my idol, the locket unfortunately fell off. He picked it up, saw his picture and burst into whoops of laughter. And that was the end of the crush.

What did it start from? Nothing more important than a ride on the back of a strange boy's bike. Actually, crushes on boys are a kind of emotional dress rehearsal. They're ways of learning about yourself and about boys and the kind you'll wind up really being able to love and have something in common with some day.

The only thing that's wrong with them is that they can get you into horribly embarrassing situations—as I discovered in l'affaire locket. The best course, I've become convinced, is to keep them to yourself as much as you possibly can. It would take superhuman will power, I imagine, not to confide in your best friend, but let's hope she's the kind you can count on to let your secret go no further.

And, no matter whom your crush is on, don't live for it alone. Make yourself do things and have good times with other people too. They last and crushes don't.

"There must be something wrong with me to be so fickle," I've heard girls say many times. "I get all wrapped up in something and then in a couple of months it bores me stiff. And I never seem to like the same boy for more than a month. Why can't I stick to my interests?"

Relax. You're experimenting, which is a very constructive thing for you to do. How else would you learn about all the interesting things and different kinds of people there are in the world? When you find the people who really appeal to you and the interests that really absorb you, it will be time enough to stick with them. And you'll be much surer you've made the right choices than you could be if you'd made up your mind firmly at twelve that there was only one way of life or one kind of friend for you.

Meanwhile, you can avoid the danger of hurting people's feelings by not letting your friendships become too intimate till you're sure you want to keep them. Don't tell every boy who takes you out that he's the one-and-only for you—even if he seems to be that particular night. Just tell him you think he's real nice and you hope you'll see him soon.

Tact is a priceless quality which the dictionary defines as: "acute discernment of what is appropriate to say and do in dealing with others; the ability to deal with others without giving offense or so as to win good will, especially in difficult situations."

Unhappily, it's not an ability we're necessarily born with, as the social gambits of the average four-year-old make abundantly clear. "Why do you have such a funny nose?" or "My Mother was hoping you wouldn't be able to come" are fairly typical examples. Sometimes the tactlessness of children is funny; more often it's excruciatingly embarrassing for Mother or whatever adult is involved. When the company has departed little

Suzy is likely to be treated to a sound walloping or an impassioned lecture from Mother on the necessity for not saying the first thing that comes into her head.

But poor Suzy's mistake is an honest one; she hasn't lived with other people long enough to be able always to "discern what is appropriate to say and do," and because she finds the guest's nose or unwelcomeness interesting, she believes everyone else must too.

By the time Suzy is in her teens, she usually has learned a good deal more about what is appropriate and what isn't, but sometimes she still finds herself "putting her foot in it," often to her own embarrassment as much as anyone else's. My advice to Suzy is to try, and keep on trying, to think before she speaks, to take a moment to reflect how the remark she's about to make would strike *her* if someone else said it, or to think about why she is going to make it.

Sometimes people are tactless simply because they remain as straightforward as a child all their lives and have never learned the importance of not saying everything that comes into their heads. Sometimes their tactlessness reflects a lack of understanding of people and their feelings. We've all known tactless people, and though we may learn to love them for their other qualities, we're apt to agree that in social situations they are pretty hard to take.

One of the most valuable social graces to learn, I'd say is: How to keep your foot out of your mouth, or Think before you speak! But if you make the occasional boner, don't brood over it too long or decide you're washed up socially. Every one of us has made one, and probably will again.

Learning to refrain from gossip takes much more will power, I'll admit—and admit too that it's a rare soul who has a completely clean slate on this score. But a clean slate is certainly worth working for, not only because of the damage and hurt that gossip can cause others, but because the person most likely to be damaged by it

in the long run is the gossiper herself. It takes no time at all for people to "spot" her, and then all but the most unwary are on their guard whenever they're with her. "For Heaven's sake, don't tell Alice," they say, "she'll have it all over town in a minute." Pretty soon, poor Alice is lucky if she can find someone who's willing to tell her what day of the week it is.

Gossiping is hard to resist because it seems fun, or exciting, or because it makes you feel important or more in the know than anyone else. But its rewards are meager and quickly over. And it's much more flattering to have a reputation for being someone who can always be trusted with a confidence.

I hope now that when you look into your mental mirror, you'll be able to see a little more clearly who you are and to realize that you're neither all good nor all bad, that there are some things—like being tall or being

gossip.

short—you can't change and shouldn't try to. They're you. If you accept the fundamentals in good spirit and spend your time working on the things you *can* change, you're on your way to being the kind of girl you admire most.

11. In Social Situations

▶ *What Manners Are*

The thousands of little social customs we live by may seem silly and artificial at times. What's the *point* in a man letting me go first through a door, or why *should* I stand up when an older person comes into the room? You may wonder. But once you stop to think about their reason for being, they make perfectly good sense.

Actually, the foundation of what we call "good manners" is very simple: consideration for the feelings of other people. And obviously, life will be pleasanter for everyone, and people will find each other easier to get along with, if they are considerate of one another. So when a young person stands up for an older one she's not simply going through meaningless motions. She is using an accepted way of showing consideration.

In the chapter on boys, I talked about the manners of date behavior. Only I didn't use the word "manners." I said, "if you want to get along with boys" or "if you want him to ask you again" . . . So you see, manners really do boil down to getting along with people comfortably and pleasantly, which is what everyone would like.

Anyone who has really absorbed this basic principle could probably find his way through most social situations, but possibly not without a few missteps and a few embarrassing moments, and that is why it's well worth while to learn the rules of the social game.

The classic boner by the guest who had never seen a finger bowl and plopped his ice cream into it while everyone else was daintily rinsing his fingers isn't as likely to be made today, but there are plenty of other social pitfalls that can make a girl wish to drop dead on the spot if she's never learned how to sidestep them. But if she *does* know how to handle herself gracefully in any situation that may arise, she'll have a head start on self-confidence that's hard to beat.

▶ Feeling at Ease with Older People

For some girls this is no problem. Possibly a lot of their childhood was spent in the company of their parents' friends and they fully believe that adults are people—and fun people to be with. For others, an adult seems such a strange and remote creature that the prospect of being trapped with one for ten minutes is enough to fairly paralyze them.

Again, the shortest road to poise in this situation is to get a firm grasp on the rules of the game. If you remember always to stand when an older person comes into the room, if you greet him courteously, listen politely to whatever he has to say, excuse yourself graciously when it is time, you'll know you're above reproach as far as you've gone. Whereas if you try to cover up your shyness or lack of poise by pretended indifference to his presence, you'll only seem more awkward to yourself and to him.

If you find yourself confronted by a stranger and there is no one handy to introduce you to him, don't stand there eying him like a grenade that might go off at any minute. If you know who he is, use his name as you hold out your hand, smile and say, "How do you do, Mr. Soandso, I'm Alice Phillips."

Incidentally, three things that can make you seem poised, even when you're quaking inside, are: a firm handshake, a friendly smile, and eyes that look at the person you are meeting.

Some time or other you may have to introduce a friend your own age to an older person—and that is just the way to do it, not the other way around—Mr. Soandso, this is my friend, Mary Jordan; *never*, Mary, this is Mr. Soandso. In the case of your parents, though, you present the stranger to them.

Conversation with adults is not always easy, I'll admit. Often they feel every bit as self-conscious with younger people as younger people do with them. And in their desperate efforts to find a conversational approach they may strike you as hopelessly patronizing or just plain square.

Here is where remembering the basic principle of good manners can ease the situation no end. Instead of barely masking your boredom or irritation or contempt, try to make an older person more at ease by making him less conscious of the gap between your generations. If you can relax and talk naturally, as you would to someone your own age, so will he—and the first thing you know you may be having a conversation that's fun for both of you.

I'd like to mention here that the rules of courtesy to adults apply equally and always to your parents. They may sometimes overlook flipness or rudeness or lack of consideration from their darlings rather than call them down in public, but believe me, the other people present never overlook such behavior and never think it's smart.

A final, and basely practical, reason for learning easy, pleasing ways with adults is that soon almost all your important dealings will be with them, whether it's college or a job you're after. No matter what it is you want, whether you succeed in getting it depends to a large extent on the social impression you make. Your courtesy and friendliness will never be wasted or go unnoticed, I promise. On this score, older people never miss a trick.

▶ Party Manners

A party calls for your prettiest face, your prettiest dress, your prettiest manners. Don't ever make the ostrich's mistake and think that the presence of a crowd ever hides an individual's behavior. No matter how many people are present, a hostess has an uncanny way of noticing who it is that carelessly flicks cigarette ashes all over her carpet or talks louder than anyone else or leaves without saying goodnight. And usually she doesn't invite that person again.

It's not hard to be a popular guest; all it takes is remembering the obligation to be a pleasant, helpful and cooperative addition to the group.

Parents often stay in the background when their sons or daughters give a party. But if you're a guest, never forget for a moment that it is *their* home the party is in and that *they* are actually your hosts. Be sure you greet them when you arrive and thank them when you leave. In the time between, be as considerate of their furniture, their belongings and their nerves as you would be of your own. Carelessness, loudness, wildness are very unsuccessful ways of showing you are having a good time.

Lateness for a meal in someone's house is inexcusable, unless you have a very good reason. So is bringing a friend or house guest to any sort of party, dinner or

other, without asking permission ahead of time. Another point—never let anyone persuade *you* to go along to a party with them unless you are quite sure they have cleared it with the hostess. You'd be too miserable with embarrassment to have any fun.

When the party is over, don't be the last one to face the fact. It's often a great temptation to put on one more record or dance one more dance, but nine times out of ten the temptation would vanish quickly if you could read your hostess' mind.

▶ When You're the Hostess

Your main objectives are to see that your guests have a good time—and to have one yourself. You'll accomplish both best if you can relax. Remember that the party is for fun and not to show off your mother's best china or your new dress. If arrangements or refreshments must be simple, don't fret about it or apologize because you can't offer something fancier. Anyone would rather eat a hot dog in a relaxed atmosphere than a crêpe suzette in a strained one.

You want the confident feeling of knowing everything is prepared and you are ready to greet your guests when the hour arrives, so make sure all the details are taken care of and that you are dressed well ahead of time. It's hard to look welcoming as you greet the first arrivals when you know the cookies are burning in the oven.

It's up to you to see that everyone knows or meets everyone else at your party. The shy guest, the stranger or the lame duck are squarely your responsibility. And it doesn't end with introductions.

If you see anyone moping alone or stuck with another guest he doesn't know how to take leave of gracefully, it's you, Madam, who are supposed to fly to the rescue. Take the time to chat with him yourself for a few minutes, then see if you can't ease him into another group. When you find you have someone hopelessly shy or a complete conversational fizzle on your hands, the best way to ease his evening is to ask him to help with something—changing records, opening cokes, passing sandwiches or whatever. He'll be deeply grateful for something to do.

Refreshments will probably be on a help-yourself basis, but if you see a guest without any, make sure it is not because he or she was too shy to step up to the groaning board or didn't know where it was.

If a catastrophe occurs and your mother's best vase or Dad's favorite record is accidentally smashed, you can only do what your mother or father would do—try to help the guest over his embarrassment by taking the accident lightly. You may be quaking inside at the thought of what Mother or Dad will say tomorrow, but don't let the guest know it. He feels miserable enough already.

It's quite a different situation, though, when a party starts to get wild or out of hand. You are not expected to stand back smiling while guests turn the living room into a shambles. If you see any signs of this happening, nip them in the bud, pleasantly but firmly. Often you can ask one or two boys you can count on to help you pass the word that the joint is beginning to jump *too* much.

It's only natural that with a large group you'll be more

interested in some of your guests than others (in fact, you may secretly wish you hadn't had to invite one or two). But make sure these feelings remain a dark secret between you and yourself. One of the social obligatons you undertake when you entertain is that of doing everything in your power to insure that everyone under your roof has the best possible time.

It takes some skill and practice to navigate a party ship so that no one feels left out or uncomfortable, but it's worth the effort to know, when the evening is over, the last dish washed and your tired feet propped up at last, that everyone present went home thinking your party was the best they'd ever been to.

▶ In a Restaurant

Whether it's the corner hamburger joint or the main dining room of the Waldorf-Astoria you're headed for, you want to take your restaurant manners with you. And the fancier the place, the surer you want to be that you know how to handle any situation that might arise.

To start with the basics first, here are certain courtesies to your escort or hostess to be observed. No matter whom you're with, whether it's Dreamboat or Aunt Jane, give your entire attention to him—not to new arrivals coming in the door or to your own image in a wall mirror or, heaven forfend, to remaking your face or fussing with your hairdo.

It's customary for whoever is paying the check to give the order, and you're usually cued for this by your date asking you what you would like when the waiter comes to take the order. Unless you know that price is no object, don't order the most expensive thing in sight.

If you must freshen your make-up, the ladies' room is the only place to do anything more than dab quickly at your nose with a powder puff. But, please, make your stay there brief and go equipped with your very own quarter for the attendant. Probably the only thing that infuriates men more than sitting at a table alone for what seems hours is having to ante up a quarter for the privilege because a girl didn't think to bring any change with her.

When you leave the restaurant, even though you're going on together, say something to your host about how much you enjoyed going there or how delicious the food was. It may have seemed like Sloppy Joe's to you, or the dish you ordered may have been a total flop, but obviously the person who took you there chose as he did with the hope of pleasing you, so don't shatter his dream.

The date who is rude or bossy to waiters is high on the undesirable list of most men. The service may be perfectly abominable, but it's never up to a guest to say so or call the waiter down. There is an old legend that it's fatal to send a dish back in a restaurant because the chef or waiter will revenge himself by substituting something even worse or returning the original dish in sadder shape than it was to begin with. I suspect this is a slight exaggeration, but I wouldn't make the mistake of sending something back unless the waiter has really brought the wrong order or one that's not fit to eat. And, in any case, be pleasant about the whole thing. The waiter then is more likely to be, too.

Menus in the more sophisticated restaurants may look as though they were written in Egyptian the first time you encouner them, but translation is not impossible if you know the key words. Most of the standard ones are French: *à la carte* means that each item on the menu is individually priced; *table d'hôte* means that the price listed covers the entire meal. *Hors d'oeuvres* are appetizers—shrimp, perhaps, or marinated vegetables or celery and olives; the *entrée* is the main dish. If entrèe, dessert and coffee is as much as you feel like eating, don't hesitate to say so. On the other hand, if you order only a soup or appetizer and dessert you may provoke some odd looks from the waiter. *Demitasse* is, of course,

French for a half cup, in this case a small after dinner cup of coffee, which is always drunk without milk or cream.

When there are dishes listed that are utterly strange to you, there's no shame at all involved in sweetly asking the waiter to describe them to you. In their attempts to make the same old meat and potatoes sound exotic, restaurants sometimes go to extraordinary lengths in naming their dishes.

After you've successfully negotiated the ordering of your meal, there may still be a booby trap or two in eating it gracefully. The main one is: which foods may be eaten with the fingers and which call for a knife and fork?

Here is a list of the accepted finger foods: potato chips, shoestring potatoes (crisp), celery, olives, radishes, corn on the cob, any sort of bread except spoon bread (which is more like a pudding), sandwiches which are neither drippy nor double-decker, wedges of cheese, whole fruits such as bananas, apples, pears, grapes, and artichokes.

That last vegetable, by the way, may seem very mysterious to manage, but it really is not. Peel off the outer leaves one by one with your fingers, dip the stem end into a little side dish of sauce (which may be melted butter, mayonnaise or French dressing), and bite it off, discarding the rest of the leaf on the side of your plate. (Usually, only about a third of the leaf is tender enough to eat.) When you get to the center of the vegetable you'll see the choke that gives it its name. This is a crown of tiny spines (and they do choke you —I once tried them) which you scrape away with your knife and fork to reveal the artichoke's reward—the heart, which is the tenderest, sweetest part, a real delicacy. It's too big for one mouthful, so you cut it up and use your fork to dip the pieces in sauce and put them in your receptive mouth.

Fried chicken, lamb chop bones, asparagus spears,

bacon strips and French fried potatoes are perfectly all right as finger foods at home if you prefer, but in a restaurant, knife and fork is the rule. So much for fingers.

Italian spaghetti presents a challenge all its own. It takes some practice and dexterity to wrap those long slithery strands around your fork without leaving a lot of loose ends dangling. If you haven't mastered the technique, help yourself by resting the prongs of the fork in the bowl of a dessert spoon as you wind. Or use your fork to cut the spaghetti into more manageable lengths.

The rule on cake is: if it's fairly firm and not iced, pick it up in your fingers. If it's soft, sticky or gooey you'll manage much less messily with a fork.

Some general do's and don'ts:

• Tea or coffee spoons are never left in the cup. They go in the saucer when not in use.

NO

• Never blow on soup or coffee to cool it. Wait a minute.

NO

• No matter how hungry you are, don't bolt your food. (Bad for your digestion, anyway, as well as being bad manners.)

• One elbow may be leaned gracefully on the table between courses. Both elbows on the table when you're eating are taboo.

• Dunking and crumbling crackers into soup are habits to keep at home.

• Bread is buttered, a bit at a time, breaking off a bite-size piece as you're ready to eat it.

• A soup bowl is always tipped away from you, not toward you, when you're down to the last few mouthfuls.

• Saucers, edges of plates, dregs of coffee (horrors!) are not the right receptacles for cigaret butts. When you don't see an ashtray, ask for one.

▶ *When You're a Guest in the House*

Being a guest can be loads of fun, and you'll probably be one often if you make your visit an equal pleasure for the family you are staying with.

The trick to that is keeping your standard of manners and consideration just a little higher than it is at home (unless you're an absolute paragon!) while at the same time you show your hosts that you feel quite at home with them.

Most essential, of course, is not to cause extra work or inconvenience for anyone in the family you are visiting. Keep your room in apple-pie order; don't hog the family bathroom or leave it looking like a battle site; be punctual for meals and show your appreciation of them; fall in cheerfully with whatever plans have been made for you. And, unless the friend you are visiting is one who just loves lending her best sweater or new skirt, be sure you bring the clothes you'll need with you. The guest who has to be clothed as well as sheltered and fed is a nuisance to have around.

You can show that you feel at home by being as helpful as you would be in your own family. Offer to help with table-setting and dishwashing (unless there's a maid), or to mind the baby for an hour or to run down to the store if something is needed. If you keep your eyes open you'll see lots of ways to be helpful, and if your offer is made naturally and sincerely it will probably be gratefully accepted.

Write your bread-and-butter letter the *minute* you get home. A good way to pass the time on the return trip is

to compose it mentally—while your enthusiasm is still
fresh. There is no rigid form that a thank-you letter
must take, nor need it be long. What's really important
is to sound sincere and spontaneous in your appreciation and not as though you were being forced to
write "I will not be late for school" a hundred times on
the blackboard.

Your letter of thanks (to the mother of your friend)
might go like this:

Dear Mrs. Grant,

My week visiting Jean was so much fun, I'm still
on Cloud Nine. Thank you for your big part in it
and for making me feel so welcome and comfortable.
I thoroughly enjoyed our sightseeing tour of the city
—Mr. Grant was a wonderful guide! And I've been
pestering Mom ever since I got home to let me try
making your popovers for our Sunday-dinner company.

Next time the Grants come to our part of the country, please stop in to see us, and I hope you'll let Jean
visit me sometime very soon. Thanks again.

Sincerely,

▶ If You're Job Hunting

Whether you're simply out for a pin-money job after
school or on the brink of what you hope will be a career,
the way you go after it has almost everything to do
with your success. Prospective employers are very likely
to turn thumbs down on a girl who hasn't taken the
trouble to get a working knowledge of business manners, even though she may be perfectly competent in
other respects.

The accepted procedure when you are job hunting is:
write to the executive in whose department you hope
there may be an opening, or telephone his secretary

and ask for an appointment. If you don't know the name of any person, apply to "personnel."

If you write, be sure the letter is typewritten *perfectly* (even if it means retyping it six times), brief and to the point, that your signature is legible and your address and telephone number clearly evident. If you have never worked before, you haven't anything to put in a résumé, so simply state in your letter your age, where you are at school and in what way you think you might be helpful to the company. If you *have* had some previous experience, list it in chronological order on a separate sheet of paper, along with a record of the school or schools you have attended and any extra-curricular activities that are pertinent. In your letter, mention that *your* résumé is attached. Your letter of application for a job should look like this:

> 2001 First Avenue
> New York 28, New York
> May 1, 19—

Mr. Charles Darwin
The Acme Dress Corporation
12 Seventh Avenue
New York 2, New York

Dear Mr. Darwin:

Mr. Gilbert Hoit suggested that you might be in need of a receptionist as a summer replacement for one of your employees, and I would like to apply for the job.

I am a sophomore at Manuel Erasmus High School, 83rd Street and West End Avenue, and have been taking a course in typing and shorthand in the evenings. Last summer I worked as a receptionist for Mr. Hoit on Saturdays, so I am acquainted with some of the people who might come to your office. I am very much interested in the fashion industry and hope to make it my career when I graduate from school.

I would like to come in for an interview, and will telephone your secretary to ask when is most convenient for you.

Sincerely yours,

If you telephone, instead of writing first, don't try to keep the executive's secretary in the dark as to what you want or insist on speaking to the man himself. You'll never get a chance to. Instead, explain to her what sort of job you are looking for, what your qualifications are and any special reason you have for approaching her boss. Ask her to tell you when you may come in for an interview.

When that great day comes, be sure you're neatly and appropriately dressed—heels, a hat, purse and clean gloves are musts—that you are discreetly made up and that you are right on time. Nothing is quite so infuriating to a busy businessman as to have a tight work schedule bolloxed up by a stranger.

Bring a résumé with you, if you have one, and hand it

to him as quickly as possible. It may save time for both of you.

It's nice (though not easy) to look relaxed, but don't go so far in your efforts that you lounge in your chair or perch on a corner of his desk or chew thoughtfully on a stick of gum.

Don't volunteer information that hasn't anything to do with the job, but be quick and cooperative with your answers to any questions he may ask. He's not going to be favorably impressed if he has to wring each small item of information out of you.

Don't drag out an interview in the hope of catching the interest of someone who seems uninterested. And when it is over, thank both the person you've seen and his secretary for their courtesy—even if both of them have been cold as cucumbers and you'd like to wring their necks!

Unless you have been told at the outset that there is no opening, the prospective employer will probably say that you will hear from him in a few days. Give him a week. After that, it is perfectly permissible to telephone his secretary and ask if any decision has been made about the job. She may tell you that they are still interviewing or that her boss is out of town but that you're still in the running. Don't push her, but do say pleasantly that you hope they can give you an answer soon because summer vacation is short and you are anxious to make the most of it. If, within a few more days, you've still had no word, you might as well mark this company down as having business manners nowhere near so good as yours, and try somewhere else. Happy hunting!

► *About Letters*

As with every other kind of social communication, there are some rules about correspondence that are valuable to remember. The most important ones are:

Simple writing paper is considered in better taste than

paper embellished with hearts and flowers or other cute decorations. Wild colored inks, writing diagonally across the paper, and so forth, also mark the writer as definitely "younger set."

Business letters should always be typewritten; personal letters should never be, unless they are completely informal ones to an intimate friend.

With writing paper that is not marked with name and address, the writer's address is placed in the upper right-hand corner of the page with the date just below it.

▶ Letters for Special Occasions

A letter of thanks for a gift:

February 31, 19—

Dear Aunt Isabelle:

You've made me your willing slave forever (though really, I already was) with that perfectly beautiful birthday blouse. If you're not psychic, how did you know the color is exactly right for my new suit. Thank you, thank you, thank you!

One bit of family news: I've finally broken down Mother's resistance to dogs, and the newest addition to the household is a three-months old cocker spaniel named Tippy. I'm mad for him, and secretly so is Mother, I believe.

When are we going to see you? Soon, I hope.

Affectionately,

Reply to an informal invitation:

February 31, 19—

Dear Janet:

I'm terribly disappointed that I won't be able to come to your surprise party for Peggy. That's the week end that Mother and Dad have been planning to take us all to West Point—a long-anticipated outing.

Will you tell Peggy how sorry I am to miss seeing her? I know the party will be a huge success.

Affectionately,

Letter of congratulation:

February 31, 19—

Dear Bob:

I've just heard about your winning the Thayer Scholarship and couldn't wait to tell you what wonderful news I think that is. We were all rooting for you, but it was your hard work that did the trick! I can't think of anyone who deserves the Thayer more.

Cordially,

Letter of condolence:

February 31, 19—

Dear Mary:

I was so terribly sorry to hear the sad news about your mother. She was always wonderfully sweet and welcoming to all your friends, and all of us will miss her a great deal.

If there is anything at all I can do to make things easier for you, will you let me know?

Affectionately,

12. It Pays to Be Informed

Never be afraid to use your head. A lot of girls are. They think they might be considered longhair or square. They believe that old saw that boys are frightened of girls with brains, or, as Dorothy Parker once put it, "Men never make passes at girls who wear glasses," which couldn't be further from the truth. Or perhaps they're scared off by that other old fallacy—that anyone who is "different" from the rest of the group, who knows more, reads more, has more varied interests or an appreciation of such things as music or books or art is automatically a weird-o and doomed to pursue those interests in lonely grandeur.

To prove it, they can usually point to a horrible example somewhere on the fringe of the group—an unpopular, not-too-attractive girl who is so immersed in her special interests that everyone assumes she doesn't care about anything else and leaves her strictly alone.

There are several things wrong with this picture. The sad example of the isolated egghead, for instance, probably puts the cart before the horse. She isn't unpopular

168

because she is brainy; it is because she's unpopular that she *is* so intensely intellectual. Having realized that for one reason or another—looks or personality or maybe just shyness—she isn't going to get much attention or satisfaction from the group, she has made up for it by getting satisfaction from other sources. And very wise she is, too, for later on she will meet a lot of other people just like herself. With the background of interests she has amassed during these early, lonely years, she will fit in with them very well, and win the admiration and interest that everyone wants so much.

But at the same time, here *is* one thing she is making a mistake about, and it's nine-tenths responsible for the way people feel about her. It isn't *what* she knows, it's the way she lets people know she knows. You can't really blame her; people who score low on the beauty-personality scale are naturally tempted to show off intellectually just to prove that there is something in which they're tops. Unfortunately, instead of being better liked for their brains, they are liked even less—not because they're bright but because they make everyone else feel stupid. The fault is with personality, not intellect.

A widespread and completely mistaken idea is that beauty and brains don't go together. Actually, they seem to be handed out to the population at random. Some lucky people get a high degree of both. Most of us get a mixed helping with enough of each to get along. It's true, perhaps, that some people, born extra-beautiful, find life so easy and fall so much in love with themselves that they never bother to develop what brains they have. But the fact remains that an empty head never made anyone's features more attractive.

On the other hand, a lively, hard-working mind can, in a subtle way, make a girl seem more attractive, to say nothing of making her better company.

Some people think that an actress, for instance, succeeds on looks alone. It just isn't so. There is no such thing as a really successful actress who has not only brains but a burning desire to use them and a capacity for the endless hard work that goes into learning any art, or even trade.

Whatever you want to be, you'll go further and get there faster if you have learned to use your mind. This doesn't come entirely naturally, I must add. It's hard work, but any kind of work becomes easier with practice. Ballet dancers, for instance, must start at the age of nine or ten to learn the discipline of dancing and to develop their muscles. In four or five years they are able to do easily things that are completely impossible for the untrained. You can train your mind in much the same way, and it will respond just as beautifully.

At this point, you may be asking plaintively what I'm talking about, anyway. If you're doing well in school, what more are you expected to learn. The answer is: Plenty! As much as you can about as many things as you can. None of it will ever be wasted, and the ways it can make life more successful, more glamorous and more fun are too many to count, but let's try.

First of all, let's hope you have ambitions. Even if you haven't yet a completely definite idea of what you would like to become or the life you would like to lead, let's assume it is something special. And let's hope too that along with wanting to be something special, you believe you may achieve it.

If so, now is the time to get going, perhaps the only time. In the case of a great many careers, ten years from now would be too late to start. The world is littered with people who mourn the careers they might have had— "If I'd only known about it sooner." Whereas almost everyone who is a success in some interesting field began when he was in his teens—if not to learn *how* to do something, at least to learn enough about the subject to know it was what he wanted.

And what about the girl who is planning marriage rather than a career? you may be asking. Well, in the first place, a career or an interest in one often determines the kind of man a girl marries. If she has no particular interests or skills she is likely to be attractive only to men who also have no interests or skills.

It's well known that in order to marry an interesting man you first have to meet him. So, if you have dreams of marrying a certain sort of man—a doctor or business-man or explorer, for instance—the fulfillment of your dreams will depend on your opportunities of meeting him, and those will depend on what you do now that might bring you into his world.

Aside from the major question of career and marriage, there's another reason to learn all you can about every-thing you can. The sum total of a person's knowledge, on subjects large and small, determines the degree of what is sometimes called the "culture" they possess. Once only the lucky few had a chance to learn much about the world outside their own back yard. Nowa-days there are opportunities for almost anyone to learn about almost anything.

Culture means having at least a passing acquaintance with such things as art and music, literature and the manners and customs of people who live differently from the people in your daily circle. It means knowing the difference between symphonic music and jazz, knowing how to order in a French restaurant or how to behave at a formal dinner party. Possessing this knowledge doesn't make a person an egghead, and it can be end-lessly useful both in serious ways and in the small change of life's pleasures.

The more things you are familiar with and can talk about, the more different kinds of people will find you interesting and attractive. Suppose a new boy comes to town and cuts in on you at a dance. You say: "How do you like the music?"

He says: "Fine, but I'm a longhair myself. I'm nuts about Debussy."

You say: "Oh, really. What's that?"

He says: "Debussy was a French composer. I only meant I like serious music. I'm planning to be a pianist."

That conversation never got off the ground, and at the first chance, the new boy cuts in on another girl.

She says: "How do you like the music?"

He says: "It's fine. Actually, though, serious music is my stuff."

She says: "Really? Mine too. I've just started learning somthing about classical music. Mozart is my man!"

He says: "Mine too! Maybe you'd like to hear some of my records? Tomorrow evening be okay?"

That illustration may seem a little over-simplified, but it really isn't far-fetched. Many a beautiful friendship has either blossomed or been nipped in the bud by conversations very much like these.

If by now I have succeeded in convincing you of the case for culture, you may ask how you're supposed to go about acquiring it. The number one way is to read. Read everything that comes your way. Read for fun.

Read novels old and new. Read newspapers and magazines. Read school books. Anything you read is adding to your culture, your store of general information. But do make sure your reading is varied. Don't read only novels, or only magazines.

Try to read at least a little about as many subjects as

you can discover. A fine way to gain background in the arts is to read the biographies of great artists—dancers, musicians, painters, poets. Read non-fiction, too. Try books, even though they may look dull or complicated, to see if they really are. It's perfectly reasonable to say you hate spinach, provided you've tasted it, but otherwise it makes no sense. It's the same with the multitude of subjecs about which books and magazine articles are written. Give them a try before you turn them down.

If you live anywhere near a city that has concerts or theaters or art museums or dance recitals, go to at least one of each before you give up. You may not like it at all, but at least you will know what it is about. And remember that the more you have read about any of those things before you go, the more chance there is that you will enjoy them when you do.

In addition to storing up general knowledge, now is also the time to learn as many skills as you can. In other words, learn not only to appreciate things but learn how to do things that are out of the general run. This could include such everyday skills as cooking, sewing or using a typewriter.

If you learn them well now, you'll always be glad you have them. And when a chance to learn a new skill comes your way, grab it. Try, at least, all the art and craft classes that are offered at your school. Don't be sure you can't draw or sing or act until you've tried. You may not turn out to be Helen Hayes or Picasso or even Doris Day, but you'll have added something to your knowledge that you'll enjoy for the rest of your life.

You know the old maxim, "Travel is broadening"? There's only one thing wrong with that truism—it neglects to mention that travel is fun, more fun than almost any other recreation and *most* fun when you're young.

If you wait till you're thirty or forty or fifty to see what the rest of the world looks like and how the rest of the population lives, you'll be too habit-ridden to enjoy it to the fullest. I'll never forget the very nice middle-aged woman I fell into conversation with on my fist trip to Chicago. I was excited to death at the thought of seeing the great city, and she was delighted to be able to tell me all the things I shouldn't miss. Then we started talking about travel in Europe; her husband had wanted to go for fifteen years and they'd just come back. Her pleasantest memory was the American ship she came home on, because she was able to get her breakfast coffee the way she was used to it! The saddest part was that she knew it was pathetic too.

Now is certainly the time to think of roaming, for dozens of reasons: you have the time—summer vacations, and they don't last forever; you're not tied down by children or a job; you have the energy to make every moment count; you have the curiosity about life, and you probably have a better background knowledge, thanks to your school work, than you'll have ten years from now, when ancient Greece or the noble Romans will seem very remote.

Finally, there are more opportunities for you to travel economically both in this country and foreign countries than there will be when you are older. All sorts of organizations work to make travel inexpensive and rewarding for boys and girls in their teens, on the sound theory that the more the people of the world know and understand one another, the better chance they have of resolving their political and national differences.

Here are some of the ways you could have a marvelous summer vacation this year:

Be a hosteler. American Youth Hostels, Inc., is a nonprofit organization devoted to helping young people learn more about the world—through travel. There are hostels in thirty-two countries, (including numerous ones in the U.S. and Canada) where members can stay overnight on trips and cook their meals. Thanks to these, a hiker or bicycling tourist can travel for as little as $2.00 a day. Youth Hostels also sponsor group tours and work-and-travel plans—wonderful ways not only to see exciting places but to meet interesting people who share your interests. The national headquarters of American Youth Hostels, Inc., is 14 West 8th Street, New York 11,

N. Y. On request, they will mail their booklet outlining requirements for hostelers (minimum age: fifteen), costs, and locations of hostels both here and abroad.

Investigate the Experiment in International Living. Every summer this organization sends groups of young people, aged sixteen to eighteen, to Austria, the British Isles, Germany, Holland, France, Mexico, Sweden or Switzerland, under the guidance of a trained leader. What is unique about the program is that each member of the group spends one month of her two-month trip living with a selected family in the country of her choice, sharing in their lives and gaining a view of the customs and a knowledge of the people that a tourist rarely has a chance to get. The second month is spent traveling with the other group members through the countryside. Like the Hostels, Experiment in International Living is co-educational. If you're interested in applying, write to Experiment in International Living, Putney, Vermont.

The American Field Service (Headquarters: 313 East 43rd Street, New York 17, N. Y.) sponsors an international student exchange program, under which American boys and girls of high school age may spend a summer living in a family in any of nineteen different countries, in exchange for their own communities providing a home for a foreign student in return. From the Field Service, you can obtain full details on the requirements for becoming a candidate for their programs.

There are many more groups. Among them:

The American Friends Service Committee (The Quakers) (New York office: 2 W. 20th Street, New York 11) which has yearly work-and-study programs for teenagers, both here and abroad.

Local branches of the Lions' Clubs, Rotary Clubs, National 4-H Clubs, YWCA, YMCA, YMHA, and U. S. Junior Chambers of Commerce.

Why not start saving and planning now for the biggest adventure of your life?

By now, you must have realized that basically I'm a Johnny One-Note, and the tune I've been warbling all through this book is a simple one: if there are things that displease you about your looks, yourself, your life, don't sit around bemoaning them. Change them. All you need is will power and know-how. You have the will power and I hope I've supplied the know-how, or some of it, at least.

So now you've read my message and it's time to close the cover and get to work. The best of luck!

Index

Index

181